THE HOSPITAL OF ST CROSS AND ALMSHOUSE OF NOBLE POVERTY

THE HOSPITAL OF ST CROSS

and Almshouse of Noble Poverty

Text and Photographs
by John Crook FSA

ISBN 978-0-9566050-0-9

Printed by Short Run Press Ltd., Exeter (www.shortrunpress.co.uk)

FOREWORD

The Hospital of St Cross is an extraordinary rarity, a medieval settlement still standing serene in its antique river landscape. Old limestone walls rise majestic across the meadows. A Norman cruciform church is attended by a cluster of fifteenth-century living quarters, their stone chimneys rising like stovepipe hats round a spacious quadrangle. They are a reminder that welfare in the middle ages was no less comfortable for being the result of private charity.

More remarkable, St Cross retains the essentials of its twelfth-century charitable foundation, together with the later concept of 'noble poverty', both still enshrined in the brothers who occupy its rooms. There is something supremely easeful in this fusion of faith, charity, community and dignity at St Cross. It needs no explanation or excuse, and no state intervention. Even the old tradition of a 'dole' of free food and drink to passing wayfarers has been maintained into the age of the rambler and backpacker. The combination of staircase rooms, hall, master's house and porter's lodge forms a pattern of communal living that, even in the twenty-first century, has never been bettered. It was something the middle ages invented for all time.

Such places are beyond argument. Their survival is justification enough to protect and preserve them for ever.

Simon Jenkins

PREFACE

In this book I have attempted to relate the story of the Hospital of St Cross as much through its buildings as through written sources. It is a long history, going back to the 1130s. Of Bishop Henry of Blois's original foundation, only the church still stands, a perfect example of late Norman architecture. Its first construction is undocumented, and its chronology has to be teased out from the building itself. As for the domestic accommodation that Bishop Henry provided for thirteen poor men, it has vanished. The early history of the hospital as an institution rather than buildings is better recorded. Thus, we can trace with some certainty the tussle between the Knights Hospitaller, who had acquired the hospital in the mid-twelfth century, and successive bishops of Winchester.

It is fortunate indeed that the documents produced during an enquiry into the hospital's finances ordered by Bishop William of Wykeham in the late fourteenth century also contain some account of building works undertaken in his own day, notably by that influential master, John de Campeden. From these sources, and from the account rolls that occasionally survive from this period onwards, we can see how successive masters gradually established a kind of suburban manor within the precincts, complete with hall, chamber, and kitchen. The layout of the hospital was very different from what we see today.

The hospital's present layout dates from the mid-fifteenth century, when another great bishop of Winchester, Cardinal Henry Beaufort, decided to create a second institution within the precincts, originally intended to run in parallel with Henry of Blois's hospital. Alas, the revenue stream dried up soon after Beaufort's death, and his Almshouse of Noble Poverty was revived only in 1881. The thirteen original poor men moved into the accommodation that Beaufort had built for his impoverished noblemen and kinsmen, and they enjoyed the use of the former master's hall, which Beaufort had remodelled and reroofed. Later masters added their own stamp, as for example when Robert Sherborne built the ambulatory. Much reconstruction occurred in the late seventeenth century, when the works of Master Henry Compton are well documented. By then St Cross Church had long enjoyed an additional function as the parish church of the suburb of Sparkford.

The final chapters recount the Trollopian management difficulties that beset the hospital in the early nineteenth century, culminating in a famous Chancery case and the establishment of new government under a board of trustees. There followed a major refurbishment of the church and buildings by a succession of famous architects: William Butterfield, Arthur Blomfield, and Thomas Graham Jackson.

I would like to thank the brothers and staff for their interest in the project and putting up with my frequent intrusions, and I owe a particular debt of gratitude to the long-suffering porter, Catherine Secker, and her colleagues. I have had much useful discussion with Michael Carden and Dr John Hare, who have studied the hospital for many years. Thanks, too, to the Winchester Archaeological Research Group, whose excavations have added to our understanding of the hospital's development. My task would have been well-nigh impossible without Gill Rushton's detailed electronic catalogue of the hospital archives, which are deposited at the Hampshire Record Office. The Clerk to the Trustees, Piers Armstrong, has encouraged me in the writing of this book, Rosemary Andreae has been an exemplary editor, and Victoria Wakefield and her fellow Trustees have made many valuable suggestions. Finally, my thanks to Mark Couch and his colleagues at Short Run Press for producing a publication worthy of this magical place.

John Crook, *Archaeological Consultant to the Hospital of St Cross*

▲ North-east view of the hospital by Owen Browne Carter, 1839.

EXTRA PICTURE ACKNOWLEDGEMENTS AND SOURCES

Unpublished Sources: Pages **12**, **13**, **62**, **rear cover**: the watercolours by John Buckler are reproduced by kind permission of Lacewing Fine Art (www.lacewing.co.uk). Pages **x** (Winchester Bible), **50** (Godson survey), and **98** (watercolour by Richard Ubsdell) are reproduced by kind permission of the Chapter of Winchester Cathedral. Images in possession of the Hospital of St Cross are as follows: **51** (plan by Thomas E. Newton, from a lease book of 1904, privately printed for the Trustees by Warren & Son); **52** (drainage plan *c.*1880); **57** (Christmas Day 1851); **90** (Brother Bartholomew). The plan by John Carter 1789 (**93** and detail, **53**) is © The British Library. I am grateful to Peter Ferguson for his excellent reconstruction of the Renaissance choir, **75**. **Inside rear cover** (1853 plan), St Cross Archives at Hampshire Record Office, ref. 111M94W/T2/26/3.

Published sources: **3**, engraving by F. W. Fairholt, *Journal of the British Archaeological Association*, vol. 3 (1848), p. 102; **viii**, **34**, **105**, engravings after Owen Browne Carter from Milner's *History of Winchester*, 3rd edn. (1839), vol. ii, facing pp. 41 and 105, and vol. i, facing p. 129; **36**, engraving from Francis Grose's *Antiquities of England and Wales* (1783), vol. ii (kindly supplied by Philip Glassborow); **48**, engraving by William Cave from the anonymous *History of Winchester* (1773), vol. ii, facing p. 230; **73**, (Bishop Fox), Author's Collection; **86**, engraving of Brethren's Hall by W. H. Bartlett, from B. B. Woodward's *History of Hampshire* (*c.*1859), facing p. 230; **99**, portrait of Lewis Humbert, from W. T. Warren, *St Cross Hospital* (Winchester, 1899), p. 95; **101**, St Cross brothers, photo by William Savage from L. M. Humbert, *Memorials of the Hospital of St Cross* (Winchester, 1868), plate 13; **103**, St Cross brothers 1899, from W. T. Warren, *St Cross Hospital* (Winchester, 1899), p. 13.

CONTENTS

▲ A picture of Pope Desiderius in the initial letter of the prologue
to the Winchester Bible, commissioned by Bishop Henry of Blois,
is thought to have been modelled on the bishop himself.

Chapter 1

HENRY OF BLOIS AND THE CREATION OF THE HOSPITAL OF ST CROSS

The Hospital of St Cross stands to this day as the enduring memorial to one of the most powerful yet enigmatic men of twelfth-century England: Henry of Blois, bishop of Winchester and brother to King Stephen. Henry's contemporaries found him hard to classify, for he combined the qualities of a priest, statesman, patron of the arts, soldier, building impresario, and much more besides. The chronicler Henry of Huntingdon called him 'a new kind of monster . . . part monk and part knight'. The origins of some of his often contradictory characteristics may be traced in his upbringing. Born in around 1092–4, Henry was the fourth son of an Angevin nobleman, Stephen, count of Blois and Chartres, who had transformed the family's fortunes by marrying Adela, William the Conqueror's youngest daughter. Younger sons of the nobility often followed ecclesiastical careers, and as

a boy Henry was sent to the famous Burgundian abbey of Cluny, where he was professed a monk. During Henry's boyhood there, the long work of reconstructing the abbey church was coming to an end. At its consecration in 1130 Cluny's church was the largest in Christendom and arguably the finest; there can be little doubt that Henry's later career as a building bishop was a response to the splendid surroundings of his youth.

By 1126 Henry was back in England, when his uncle, King Henry I, appointed him abbot of Glastonbury, probably the youngest abbot his monks had ever known. Three years later, on 17 November 1129, Henry was consecrated bishop of Winchester, again through the king's influence. Bishop Henry was thus a powerful public figure when, on the king's death in 1135, his own brother Stephen came to the throne in the well-known coup by which the Empress Matilda was supplanted. Henry's support was essential in the success of the usurpation, though it was a decision he later regretted.

◀ HENRY OF BLOIS TRAINED AS A BOY AT THE ABBEY OF CLUNY IN BURGUNDY, AND LATER RETURNED THERE IN VOLUNTARY EXILE. HE MUST HAVE BEEN IMPRINTED WITH THE NOTION OF CLUNIAC HOSPITALITY.

1

FOUNDING THE HOSPITAL

Within a few years of his consecration Bishop Henry decided to create a charitable foundation just outside his cathedral city, an almshouse dedicated to the Holy Cross. A charming legend tells how the bishop, walking in the water-meadows south of Winchester, was encouraged to build a hospital there by a milkmaid with a pail upon her head, who opened his eyes to the poverty of the local people. The story first made its appearance in the eighteenth century and has been much embellished by subsequent re-telling: the milkmaid, for example, being identified as the Blessed Virgin Mary in disguise. The legend may indeed have been inspired by a fifteenth-century statue of the Virgin which, until it crashed to the ground in the 1750s, stood in a niche on the south side of the Beaufort Tower; her tall crown could have resembled a bucket in its weathered state.

▲ A TWENTIETH-CENTURY STATUE OF THE VIRGIN AND CHILD ON THE BEAUFORT TOWER.

The exact year when St Cross Hospital came into being is uncertain because no original documentation has survived. The best evidence is a letter from Bishop Henry to Pope Adrian IV (1154–9), copied into an early fifteenth-century register in the hospital archives. In it, the bishop claimed to have founded the hospital within three years of his consecration. That would bring the foundation date back to 1132. However, the text of the bull by which Pope Innocent II confirmed the constitution of the hospital has survived in a late fourteenth-century transcript, in which the original document was dated 10 March 1138. Even allowing for a time-lag in the correspondence with Rome, this could imply a slightly later date, say around 1135.

The practical purpose of Bishop Henry's hospital was to provide charitable support for those in financial or physical difficulty. Here he was following the example of Archbishop Lanfranc, who forty years previously had founded St John's Hospital in Canterbury, still functioning to this day on its original site under the ultimate direction of the archbishop of Canterbury, who is represented locally by a resident prior, advised by a board of trustees. Where Lanfranc got the idea for such a hospital is uncertain: there was no precedent in Normandy nor, as far as we know, in his native Lombardy.

One text has sometimes been incorrectly regarded as the hospital's original foundation document. This is the charter by which the bishop surrendered control of the hospital to the Knights Hospitaller in the 1150s. Like the other early texts, it was fortunately copied in the late fourteenth century. Bishop Henry talks of the 'hospital of Christ's poor' that he had 'newly founded outside the city walls of Winchester, for the good of his soul, and those of his predecessors and the kings of England'. This, of course, was the main purpose of the institution. Bishop Henry stresses that the hospital had been established for the good of souls: his own, those of his kinsmen, and those of the kings of England, to whom he was related. In those uncertain days it was perhaps prudent to make an early down-payment to the heavenly insurance policy, though founding charitable institutions was something churchmen usually did as death approached, and Henry was only in his forties.

◀ An image of Henry of Blois, *Henricus Episcopus*, holding a book or shrine panel, from a Mosan enamel plaque in the British Museum.

In a significant section of the charter, which was perhaps copied from the lost foundation deed, the bishop spelled out the hospital's practical purpose. It was to meet the needs of

> Thirteen poor men who are so feeble and lacking in strength that they can scarcely if at all look after themselves without the help of others. They are to live constantly in the said Hospital, the necessary clothing being provided for them by the head of the said house and suitable beds for those who are ill. Each day they will receive a loaf of good wheat bread weighing five measures, three dishes for dinner and one, appropriate to the day, for supper, and sufficient drink. But if it should happen that the situation of any of them improves, he should be dismissed with due honesty and reverence and replaced by someone else.

The tally of thirteen poor men was presumably inspired by the number of Christ and his apostles and was something of a commonplace in medieval Europe. Bishop Henry's munificence went further. As well as thirteen poor men, one hundred others, 'the most needful that could be found', were to be clothed and taken in for a noontide meal; they were to receive 'a loaf of the coarser sort of bread, a plate of food appropriate to the day, and a cup of the same measure', and they were allowed to take away any left-overs. All this would be funded by revenue from some of Bishop Henry's episcopal estates.

Given the bishop's insistence that the primary aim of the hospital was the spiritual benefits that it would bring to his soul and those of his predecessors and relations, it would be interesting to know whether he envisaged that it might also function as a chantry chapel or college. The size of the church as eventually built supports this idea. In 1367–74, when Bishop William of Wykeham's lawyers were trying to ascertain the hospital's primary purpose during a protracted lawsuit over alleged financial mismanagement by the master, it was again claimed that the duty of the thirteen poor men was to 'pour out prayers to the Almighty for the souls of Henry of Blois, his predecessors, and the kings of England'. This was, however, a contemporary interpretation, not based on any of the surviving twelfth-century texts. A chantry college would probably have comprised more than thirteen poor men, but we do not know the size of the original foundation. The earliest reliable staff lists date from the 1390s, by which time there were a master, a steward, four chaplains, thirteen clerks (adult singers), seven choristers, plus an army of servants: four 'servers', two servants, three bakers, three brewers, a cook, a groundsman, two grooms, and three cart drivers. It would be unwise to conclude however that this was the original foundation, and the twelfth-century hospital may have been far more modest.

The Setting

St Cross must boast one of the most enchanting natural settings of any medieval almshouse. It lies in the water meadows of the River Itchen, a

ST CROSS HOSPITAL FROM THE NORTH-EAST. THE HOSPITAL WAS FOUNDED AT THE START OF KING STEPHEN'S REIGN, DESCRIBED BY A CONTEMPORARY CHRONICLER AS 'NINETEEN LONG WINTERS, WHEN CHRIST AND HIS SAINTS SLEPT'.

delightful chalk stream. To the east rise the steep slopes of St Catherine's Hill; to the west is a more gentle ascent towards the heights known since the seventeenth century as Oliver Cromwell's Battery. In Roman times, a major road was established from *Clausentum* (modern Bitterne, now a suburb of Southampton) to *Venta Belgarum* (Winchester). The approach to *Venta* survives as today's St Cross Road, leading towards the Roman south gate, now represented only by the name Southgate Street. Near Winchester a second road branched off towards the Roman gate that in Saxon times became known as Kingsgate, the approach to the royal palace.

It was here, less than two miles from his cathedral and episcopal palace, that Bishop Henry acquired a piece of land as the site of his new hospital; it probably previously belonged to the cathedral priory. The area was known as 'Sparkford', a name that first appears as a personal name, Odo d'Esperchefort, living there in 1066, and the first part seems to come from an Old English word for the shoot of a tree (a sprig). Perhaps a distinctive tree indicated from afar where the Itchen, or one of its tributary streams, could be forded. A much debated question is whether the hospital replaced an earlier foundation in the same location. In 1616, Bishop Francis Godwin claimed in his biography of English bishops (*De Præsulibus*) that Bishop Henry had established his hospital on the site of 'some sort of small religious house (*cænobiolum*) which had been founded a few centuries earlier but was destroyed by the Danes'. No archaeological evidence has yet been found for such an assertion.

One might have expected that the hospital would front on to the old Roman road. In fact it is separated from it by a strip of land that remained in the hands of St Swithun's Priory; there is a similar strip north of the approach drive ('The Gravels') where the present Master's House stands. It looks as though Bishop Henry wanted to provide a buffer zone, so that the thirteen brethren would enjoy an element of seclusion, perhaps a reflection of Henry's monastic upbringing.

◀ THE VESTRY AT THE END OF THE SOUTH TRANSEPT CONTAINS A TINY FRAGMENT OF THE HOSPITAL'S EARLIEST SURVIVING STANDING BUILDING.

BUILDING THE HOSPITAL

Construction work on the brothers' accommodation must have started as soon as the hospital was established, though the present church was begun almost thirty years later. Only one fragment survives from the earlier period. At the end of the church's south transept is a low vestry, comprising two small rooms. The northernmost has a fine Romanesque rib-vault, springing from multi-scalloped capitals just above floor level. These details pre-date the rest of the church stylistically, and could well be of the 1130s; furthermore, the vestry vault is truncated by the south wall of the transept. The vault seems therefore to be a small part of an older building that was retained when the present church was started in the late 1150s. The level of the scallop capitals indicates that the building's original floor level was as much as a metre below the present floor. This suggests that what has survived may have been an undercroft; it is unlikely that it was part of an earlier church. It could have been part of cellarage for the storage of food, rather like the cellarer's range of a monastery.

At present we have no idea of what the hospital's accommodation was like in Bishop Henry's day. Although it is usually assumed that the original thirteen brothers had individual cells, it is perhaps more probable that they were housed in a single hall, along the lines of a monastic infirmary,

▼ THE VAULT OF THE VESTRY IS TRUNCATED BY THE SOUTH WALL OF THE TRANSEPT, SHOWING THAT THE VESTRY FORMS PART OF AN EARLIER BUILDING.

▼ A TWELFTH-CENTURY SCALLOP CAPITAL JUST ABOVE THE VESTRY PAVEMENT SUGGESTS THE FLOOR LEVEL WAS ORIGINALLY MUCH LOWER.

▶ A DEEP DITCH EXCAVATED IN ST CROSS PARK MARKED THE WESTERN BOUNDARY OF THE SOUTHERN HALF OF THE HOSPITAL PRECINCTS.

◀ EXCAVATED WALL FOUNDATIONS BENEATH THE BOWLING GREEN, THOUGHT TO BE THOSE OF THE EARLIEST BROTHERS' ACCOMMODATION.

perhaps with a chapel at the east end. The earliest reference to individual rooms dates only from 1390.

Archaeological excavation has unearthed possible evidence for the original brothers' lodgings. In the summer of 2009 members of the Winchester Archaeological Research Group (WARG) dug a small exploratory trench in the area called the Bowling Green, east of the church. Just below the surface they came across the footings of medieval walls, probably dating from the twelfth century. Further excavation will give a better understanding of how Henry of Blois's domestic buildings were laid out.

One other feature of the hospital may well date from Bishop Henry's day. This is the deep ditch (excavated by WARG in 2008–9) that runs southwards in St Cross Meadow, and divides the original park from a strip of land that until the early nineteenth century belonged to the cathedral. The ditch is mentioned in a document of 1404 describing the hospital's boundaries, and perhaps was originally dug in order to define the precincts, a symbol of the seclusion that Bishop Henry hoped his poor men would enjoy.

GOVERNANCE BY THE KNIGHTS HOSPITALLER

Bishop Henry could scarcely have chosen a worse time to found a charity. Within a year or two, his

brother Stephen became king, in December 1135, and the seeds of civil war were sown. The bishop supported first Stephen, then (for a short time) the Empress Matilda, then Stephen again. The long period known as the Anarchy, 'nineteen long winters, when Christ and his saints slept', came to an end with the accession of Henry II in 1154. Bishop Henry attended his coronation, but because he had abandoned the cause of the new king's mother, Empress Matilda, he prudently sought exile at Cluny between 1155 and 1158.

It was at this time, perhaps in 1158, that Henry handed over control of the hospital to the Knights Hospitaller, a religious and military order that had its origins in a hospice established in Jerusalem in around 1080. Also known as the Hospitallers of St John (and from the sixteenth century as the

◀ EVEN THE SEVENTEENTH-CENTURY LEATHER FIRE BUCKETS IN THE BRETHREN'S HALL BEAR THE BADGE OF THE HOSPITALLERS.

Knights of Malta), the order survives to this day, one of its core activities being the maintenance of St John Ambulance. The Hospitallers' control of St Cross has left its mark in the form of the cross that is the Winchester hospital's emblem. This is the Jerusalem Cross that the Hospitallers used, being the badge of the Kingdom of Jerusalem established at the end of the First Crusade. It consists of a cross with four terminal cross-bars, known as a 'cross potent', surrounded by four smaller, similar crosses. The full Jerusalem Cross may be seen in various places around the hospital, and the larger central cross potent is the silver badge worn by the hospital's 'black brothers', the heirs of Bishop Henry's original foundation.

St Cross remained under the Hospitallers' control for over two centuries; the order presumably regarded possession of the hospital as financially or politically advantageous. The disputes between the bishops of Winchester and the Hospitallers were protracted and complex. Bishop Henry's successor, Richard of Ilchester (sometimes called Richard Toclyve), sought to regain mastery of the hospital. In 1185 he succeeded in wresting back control, doubling the number of men that could claim a daily food hand-out at the hospital gate, and providing for a donation in perpetuity to the Hospitallers. He also relieved the Hospitallers of the burden of an annual rent of 10 Marks (£6.66) and two big wax altar candles to the cathedral priory, an indication that the hospital was founded on land that had originally belonged to Winchester Cathedral. Unfortunately, two years later the crusader pope Clement III was enthroned; he supported the Hospitallers' cause, as did Henry II, so control reverted to Canerius, the order's prior in England.

◀ THE JERUSALEM CROSS, BADGE OF THE KNIGHTS HOSPITALLER, IN A NINETEENTH-CENTURY WINDOW IN THE CHURCH'S SOUTH NAVE AISLE.

The Hospitallers' government received further royal endorsement on the accession of Richard the Lion-Heart. The arguments were far from settled: tensions between the bishop and the Hospitallers continued, and in 1187 a papal commission was set up to examine the matter. An attempt was made to buy off the Hospitallers, who demanded time to think things over; they procrastinated further by insisting on appealing to a more senior figure within their order, who was somewhere abroad. Of the two Hospitallers sent to find him, one never came back to England; when the other returned, he was demented. In around 1212 Bishop Peter des Roches took matters into his own hands, appointing his own master, Alan de Stoke. The pope appears to have met his match, and agreed that the appointment of the master should thereafter be done by successive bishops of Winchester. The Hospitallers were not going to give up easily, and insisted on retaining the all-important foundation documents, ensuring them a measure of control that lasted until 1379. To what extent these struggles weighed on the daily life of the thirteen poor men we cannot tell, but they certainly delayed construction of the great church which was the hospital's principal and most prestigious building.

Chapter 2

BUILDING ST CROSS CHURCH
THE FIRST PHASE, 1158–1250

The glimpse of St Cross Church that most people see through the trees as they drive northwards into Winchester might well be taken for a miniature version of the Norman tower and transept of the cathedral. A closer look soon reveals big stylistic differences between the various parts of the church. It is in fact the product of a long building process that began in the late 1150s and continued until around 1400. No records of the church's construction survive from earlier than the fourteenth century, and we have only the evidence of architectural style to provide the likely date of its various phases. The church itself is its own

▼ NORTH-EAST VIEW OF THE CHURCH, SEEN OVER ST CROSS MEADOW.

▲ STORM CLOUDS GATHER OVER ST CROSS. THE VARIATION IN THE STYLE OF THE WINDOWS IS THE FIRST CLUE THAT ST CROSS CHURCH TOOK A LONG TIME TO BUILD. FROM AFAR THE DESIGN LOOKS REASONABLY UNIFORM.

document. One thing is immediately apparent: the architectural character of even the earliest parts is too advanced to date from the 1130s, when the hospital was founded. On stylistic grounds the church was probably started *c*.1160. For the first three decades the brethren must have used either a temporary chapel or perhaps a more permanent one forming part of their lodgings.

Bishop Henry was probably reluctant to embark on the church during the turbulent period of the Anarchy, after which he was in exile at Cluny for a little over three years. We know he was back in England by 1158, when he undertook documented building works at his cathedral. This marked the start of Bishop Henry's closer involvement with the

diocese, and it was at this time that work began on St Cross Church.

The church is cruciform, with four arms extending from the central tower: a choir to the east, transepts to north and south, and a rather short aisled nave to the west. Did Bishop Henry originally hope that the nave would be longer? Certainly the present three-bay nave looks stocky compared with the spacious proportions of the rest of the building. On the other hand, the church was designed for a small community, not a parish or monastery: a large nave was not a practical requirement, however prestigious it would have appeared had it been built.

The church's design was presumably agreed between Bishop Henry and his master mason, the man who today would be called the architect. No record has survived of his identity, but design features of the earliest parts of the church suggest he was from Normandy. It is likely that Bishop Henry indicated the size and type of building

◀ THE FLAT EAST END OF THE CHURCH
WAS AN INNOVATIVE FEATURE.

he desired by referring to existing churches, and perhaps a scale model was prepared. Once the design was determined the plan would have been laid out on the ground and workmen could dig the foundation trenches.

AN ARCHITECTURAL TOUR OF THE TWELFTH-CENTURY CHURCH

The best way to understand a building is to start with the outside. Looking at the church square on from the east, one sees the earliest parts to be built: the choir with its lower, flanking aisles, and the two transepts. The east façade is typically Norman, with three levels of round-headed windows and flat pilaster buttresses. The choir's flat east end would however have struck contemporaries as an innovation; the French churches known to the master mason mostly had projecting apses. From this viewpoint one can also appreciate the variety of building stone, which gives texture and colour to the walls. The Winchester area lacks good stone, which had to be brought from afar. For the cathedral the Norman masons used Quarr stone, an excellent shelly limestone from the Isle of Wight, but by the early twelfth century the quarry there was nearly exhausted so the St Cross masons ordered limestone

from the Caen quarries of Normandy. Caen is a wonderful building stone that had been used in England eighty years previously, when Archbishop Lanfranc rebuilt Canterbury Cathedral. Bringing stone to Winchester from France differed only in degree from transporting it from the Isle of Wight: in both cases the stone had to be loaded into barges and shipped to the head of Southampton Water, and thereafter carried on carts (the Itchen was not navigable because of its many mills).

The south-east view of the church has always been popular with artists. From this viewpoint the tower dominates, mostly rebuilt in the fourteenth century, but well suited to the Norman architecture below. Here, too, there are clues to the layout of the hospital's twelfth-century domestic accommodation, especially the horizontal string-course marking the top of a vanished lean-to roof of a cloister in the angle of the transept and the choir. When the watercolourist John Buckler recorded the scene in 1829 a row of corbels once supporting the cloister roof was still visible. The reason the ground-floor windows of the two adjacent walls are so squat is because they had to peek over the cloister roof. The transept windows were later blocked, perhaps because they admitted so little light. In Buckler's watercolour the two big ground-level windows in the east end of the choir are also shown as blocked,

◀ ST CROSS CHURCH FROM THE SOUTH-EAST IN 1829 BY JOHN BUCKLER.

as they had been since around 1385 when a tall reredos was installed behind the high altar.

The raising of the choir aisle window sills was a modification (obvious inside the church), which indicates that the cloister was an afterthought. It was perhaps no more than a two-sided walkway, an agreeable place for the brethren to sit and enjoy the morning sun. It was probably also their access route into the church, through the famous 'triple arch' that is one of the building's most unusual architectural features. This probably results from a remodelling of a doorway which, for a very short time, led into the choir aisle. When the cloister was planned, the doorway was reconfigured so as to enter the transept. The recess cut into the south wall of the east arm provided a little more room for the doorway, which was elbowed into the corner by the neighbouring flat buttress on the transept wall. It was an elegant solution to a practical problem. The chief delight of the triple arch is its decoration of zig-zag chevron mouldings and foliate capitals, a foretaste of the superb decoration inside the church.

▶ ST CROSS CHURCH FROM THE SOUTH-EAST TODAY.

▲ THE TRIPLE ARCH. WATERCOLOUR BY JOHN BUCKLER, 1829.

Apart from the triple arch, the south side of the church is rather plain. This was the private side of the building; the north side, facing the main entrance, was more showy. All the windows on the north side of the choir, and the lower part of the transept (its plainer upper walls are of later date), are decorated with chevron mouldings; capitals are adorned with various kinds of foliage. The whole aspect seems calculated to impress the visitor approaching from the north.

Tucked in the corner of the north transept and choir is another blocked doorway, formerly opening into the north choir aisle. The exterior detailing is again lavish. The actual door opening is fairly narrow and slightly pointed. Around it is an outer order consisting of a wide chevron-decorated arch supported on shafts with leafy capitals. At one time there was a pentice roof over this doorway that was rebuilt more than once, as one can see from the sloping scars on the wall above it, but who might

▼ THE CHURCH FROM THE NORTH-EAST.

have used this doorway we cannot tell. Perhaps it was the original public entrance when only the choir had been built.

One other feature of the choir should be mentioned here. It is obvious that the roofs over its side aisles have been lowered; indeed, the nearly flat lead roofs are concealed behind parapets. Originally they rose steeply to the string-courses at the foot of the clerestory windows. The modification was done in the 1390s when the pointed-headed openings that originally served to light the roof-spaces from within were turned into windows to give more light to the choir from without. The heads of the window arches are just visible from afar.

▲ JAZZY CHEVRON DETAILING ON THE NORTH SIDE OF THE CHOIR, INCLUDING THE BLOCKED DOORWAY.

The architectural development of the nave is perhaps best appreciated from inside the church; we shall see that work progressed rather slowly westwards, the west front being completed only in around 1250. Thus the aisle windows in particular provide a good picture of the evolution

of English architectural style from late Norman or 'Transitional' to the first Gothic style called 'Early English'. The porch, though restored, is a splendid example of the latter. It has a fine quadripartite vault, whose central key-stone has wonderful stylised foliage. The inner doorway is particularly elegant, and retains some red paint in the deep mouldings. There would be an outcry if the stonework were painted today, but in the thirteenth century internal stonework, particularly arch mouldings, was usually brightly coloured. The builders took the opportunity of creating a chamber over the porch, with a view into the nave. This is said to have been the chaplain's lodgings, and later acquired a fireplace.

THE INTERIOR

The interior of the church immediately impresses the visitor by its height. Again, a visit should start at the east end, where the choir was the first part to be completed, required as soon as possible for the performance of the liturgy. With its interplay of round-headed and slightly pointed arches the choir is typically late Norman. The choir elevations are three-storeyed: a main arcade of slightly pointed arches (now blocked by screens) opens into the aisles; above is a triforium whose openings are framed by a lively pattern of intersecting arcading; the third level is a clerestory with a wall-passage allowing access to the windows for cleaning or repair. The choir is wonderfully luminous, not only on account of the eight windows in the east wall, but also because of the windows created at triforium level in the fourteenth century. This was done to compensate for the blocking of the two ground-level east windows at that time. When the latter windows were opened up again in the 1860s, the choir received more light than ever before.

The choir's vault is particularly impressive. It has diagonal ribs dividing each bay into four quadrants, plus an additional rib at the east end. The ribs are of stone; the vault fields between them are of chalk blocks for lightness, laid parallel to the ridge of the vault, again suggesting French design (English vaults were laid herring-bone fashion). It rises to a slight point, a feature of late Norman Transitional architecture, preparing the way for Gothic. Thus the great transverse arch

separating the two bays of the choir is also pointed. It springs from a big cluster of shafts, each of which supports some element of the vault. The shaft cluster does not go down to the ground, but ends in a plain chamfer: this treatment is reminiscent of the twelfth-century Cistercian monastery churches that Bishop Henry may have seen on his travels in France. The piers below date from the 1860s and were reinstated during the great work of restoring the church undertaken by the famous architect William Butterfield. The original piers, whose bases alone have remained, had been reinforced in the late fourteenth century by means of stone casing. Butterfield removed this, and created piers that were more in keeping with the original design.

The choir is distinguished not only by the elegance of its architectural design but also by its decoration, and perhaps the personal taste of

Bishop Henry may be discerned in this. The main motif is chevron, adorning the window arches and the vaulting ribs. Sometimes the zig-zags are in the plane of the wall, elsewhere they project forward. The other adornment is the use of foliate motifs in the capitals supporting the window arches and vaulting ribs. There are two types, both stylised. One is curly acanthus foliage, with rather windswept leaves, similar to the decoration of the contemporary Winchester Psalter and perhaps indeed inspired by manuscript drawings. The other is 'waterleaf': flat stylised foliage beloved of twelfth-century carvers. As well as these foliate types, some of the capitals are adorned with multiple scallops, a motif that made its appearance in the mid-twelfth century.

Another decorative element in the choir is the use of contrasting stone types: creamy Caen stone for the walls and the load-bearing parts of piers,

▲ The triforium and clerestory levels of the choir, showing the wonderfully inventive scheme of chevron decoration.

▲ The choir vault.

and dark Purbeck marble for the angle shafts of piers and those rising up to the vault in the corners of the choir. Purbeck marble (actually a freshwater limestone that takes a polish) was introduced to Winchester by Bishop Henry of Blois. He used it in the great hall that he built at his palace of Wolvesey, and, fittingly, for his own tomb in Winchester Cathedral. Most of the lower shafts were replaced by crinoidal limestone ones in the nineteenth

▲ A 'waterleaf' capital, typical of those used by the first master mason of St Cross Church.

▲ Twelfth-century acanthus decoration at the entrance to the north-east chapel.

17

▲ Bishop Henry of Blois's tomb in Winchester Cathedral has a lid of Purbeck marble, the decorative stone that he introduced to Winchester.

the church's first master mason; his successor, who completed the choir's central vault, was more subtle.

The choir and its aisles were probably more or less complete by Bishop Henry's death in 1171. Thereafter, with the Hospitallers controlling the funding of the enterprise, work proceeded by fits and starts, and the development of the transepts and nave was more piecemeal. Although the lower parts of both transept walls and the east bay of the nave are contemporary with the east arm, being required to buttress the tower as it rose up, the upper levels lagged well behind. The south transept was completed first, the north some time later, and the crossing tower never received the vault that was evidently intended to be supported on the great shafts running up the crossing piers.

century, but Butterfield reinstated one short length of red Purbeck marble for posterity in the north-west corner of the choir. Rather more of the original shafts seem to survive at higher level.

Coloured paint was used from the outset to provide even more adornment. There are traces of twelfth-century red and yellow foliate scroll-work in the vault fields of the north-east chapel. Some fourteenth-century tendrils possibly survive in the choir vault, but one should not be misled by the ghost outlines of a pseudo-medieval painting scheme still just discernible on some walls. It was done by Butterfield in the 1860s, but was (thankfully) removed in 1930.

The choir aisles became separate chapels in the thirteenth century but there were probably altars against the east walls from the outset. The chapels display the full repertoire of chevron vault types. They had been vaulted while the choir was still being built, and the vault is rather overpowering because the ribs are so large. This was the work of

▲ East view in the south-east chapel. An exuberant display of chevron mouldings.

THE TRANSEPTS

Compared with the choir, the south transept is disappointing: it has no aisles, little or no decoration, and is rather dark, now being lit only by two ground-floor windows on the west side, one in the gable, and four clerestory windows. Originally there were two quadrant-headed windows in the south wall, their profile determined by that of the triforium arches in front of them, but they are blocked. This transept is dominated by the nineteenth-century organ, with the choir vestry behind. The north transept on the other hand is open and spacious. The lower part of the walls is contemporary with the choir, and has similar decoration. Finest of all is the famous 'birds' beak' window on the east side. Forming a frame around the internal splay of the window is a roll moulding, over which carved eagles stretch their necks. The general concept of stylised 'beakhead' is a familiar one in twelfth-century architecture, but what is unusual about this window is that the birds are portrayed naturalistically, albeit as a repetitive pattern of identical units. In the hollows of the lozenge mouldings of the inner arch order of this window red paint is still visible: originally the window would have been brightly coloured, and the birds were probably painted as well.

The adjacent window, closer to the tower, is interesting because its splay is not symmetrical

▲ THE SOUTH TRANSEPT VIEWED FROM THE TOWER CROSSING.

◀ THE CROSSING SEEN FROM THE NORTH TRANSEPT.

▲ THE NORTH TRANSEPT.

▲ THE BIRDS' BEAK WINDOW IN THE NORTH TRANSEPT, ANOTHER INSPIRED DESIGN FROM THE 'FIRST CHOIR MASTER'.

fall on a statue of the Blessed Virgin Mary that was supported on a corbel on the second nave pillar from the crossing. What has not been noted is that the corresponding window in the south transept (now blocked) is also skewed. This was undoubtedly done because the two windows are tucked so far into the corners between the transepts and the east arm that, had they been straight, much of the light from outside would have been obscured by the choir walls. The place where the sun's rays fell on the two church festivals, which are roughly the same period from the equinox, was no doubt later noticed, and the corbel was inserted into the pillar in the thirteenth century, a hundred years after the windows were built.

In the north transept, construction seems to have paused for some time once the lower storey windows had been set in place. When work resumed, it was supervised by yet another master mason. His design, though in some ways a compromise, is

▲ LATE THIRTEENTH-CENTURY CORBEL ON A PILLAR OF THE NORTH NAVE ARCADE. IT IS STRUCK BY THE SUN'S FIRST RAYS ON HOLY CROSS DAY.

but angled southwards. Local folklore claims that it was thus built so that on two feast-days in the year, the Annunciation (25 March) and Holy Cross Day (14 September), the sun's first rays would

◀ A MAJOR DESIGN CHANGE: THE DOUBLE-HEIGHT CLERESTORY IN THE NORTH TRANSEPT, WITH THE EARLIER CLERESTORY PASSAGE NOW ENDING IN MID-AIR.

than the south. The design change did, however, lead to a rather strange effect where the clerestory passages from the choir and the east bay of the nave end in mid-air.

There are some indications of economy, notably the construction of the vault. In the choir and south transept the vault fields were constructed of square chalk blocks. But for the north transept vault the builders simply used lumps of chalk, laid as rubble over centering, and then plastered and painted with fictive joints.

THE NAVE

The east bay of the nave was built in the late twelfth century and is still Romanesque in style, and the first pair of pillars have typical twelfth-century scallop capitals. Above the slightly pointed main arch, the middle storey of this bay is blank, but the ghosts of blocked openings are visible; these gave access to the rood loft from the aisle roof spaces (where their round-headed arches are still visible) but were blocked at the Reformation. The clerestory in this bay was probably not completed. Perhaps the side walls were simply taken high enough to provide some abutment to the tower.

more successful than that of the south transept. He decided to dispense with the three-storey elevation found in the choir in favour of a two-storey elevation of main windows and clerestory alone. This permitted much bigger upper windows, making the north transept considerably lighter

◀ THE PROGRESSION OF STYLES WITHIN THE NAVE: LEFT, A TWELFTH-CENTURY SCALLOP CAPITAL; CENTRE, A 'BELL' CAPITAL OF THE THIRTEENTH CENTURY.

The style of the stocky nave pillars changes as one works westwards, and there appears to have been a break in construction, perhaps whilst work was completed in the north transept. The resumption of work is indicated by a foliate motif on the string-course above the arcade, as if the mason wished to make a clear distinction between his work and that of his predecessors. When work resumed, the new pillars had moulded 'bell capitals', a feature of the Early English style, and the leaf spurs at the corner of the pier bases are also typical of the thirteenth century. Comparison with better dated buildings suggests that the west end of the church was reached by 1250. The west doorway has, on the outside, the characteristic nailhead decoration of that period. The aisle vaulting is also of thirteenth-century type apart from the east end of the north aisle, which had been vaulted in the twelfth century.

In this thirteenth-century building campaign the main arcades of the two western bays of the nave were constructed, the aisles were vaulted, and the west doorway was completed. Then work came to a halt yet again; the thirteenth-century masonry in the two west bays goes up no further than the string-course above the main arcade. These two bays, and possibly the whole nave, were then simply covered by a temporary thatched roof, probably very low pitched and supported on temporary side walls, perhaps of timber. The thatch remained in place until 1335–45, when Master William of Edington constructed the present upper walls and built the clerestory, the upper row of windows that are seen today. The nave must have been dark indeed, little more than a building site, for there would have been no clerestory, and no west window. The present west window could only be inserted once the side walls of the nave had been completed in the 1330s.

There is no evidence that (whatever Bishop Henry's original intentions) the early thirteenth-century builders intended the nave to be longer than it is today, and in 2009 the massive footings of the big western buttresses taking the thrust of the nave arcades were excavated archaeologically. Their date was confirmed by the discovery of a silver penny of King John on top of the yellowish mortar spreads that formed whilst the west front was being built.

So, once again, the construction of the church was halted for around eighty years. That things took so long is again a reflection of the broader history of the hospital as an institution, as we shall now see.

◀ A thirteenth-century pier base on the north side of the nave. It has foliate spurs at the corners.

Chapter 3

DISPUTES AND DEVELOPMENTS
1250—1383

Given the protracted arguments between successive bishops of Winchester and the Hospitallers, it is surprising that progress on the church occurred at all. The nave had reached its full length by around 1250, but was unsuitable for worship, its half-built main elevations protected by straw. In 1255 Bishop Ethelmar de Valence appealed for funds to permit the construction work to continue. His appeal does not appear to have been successful.

During this period, in around 1275, the church's most significant wall painting was created. A niche in the south transept was decorated with two rows of painted arcades. The upper register showed scenes from the martyrdom of St Thomas Becket; the lower depicted Christ's Passion with the Crucifixion at the centre. The painting must have formed the reredos to an altar within the niche. It is in poor condition, but it is fairly easy to make out the altar with Becket's mitre on it, and a knight bringing his sword down on the kneeling archbishop's head.

At the end of the thirteenth century the first master was elected for whom there is tangible evidence. His name is known only in its Latin form, *Petrus de Sancto Mario* (Saint-Maur in France), a name best anglicised as Peter Seymour. He was previously archdeacon of Surrey, then in the Winchester diocese. Peter died in 1295 and was buried within an alcove in the north aisle of St Cross Church. His Purbeck marble coffin was opened in the early nineteenth century, and in 1868 Master Humbert recorded that 'within the recollection of a lady yet alive' his predecessor's body was seen incorrupt, 'even the features perfect'. On exposure to air, the corpse 'crumbled into dust'. Probably, as with the medieval saints' legends that lie at the heart of this kind of anecdote, the good lady's memory had embellished the tale. Nevertheless, this is the earliest identifiable tomb in the church, and a fine architectural feature. The present inscription, carved on the modern coffin lid

▶ A WALL PAINTING IN THE SOUTH TRANSEPT, SHOWING THE MARTYRDOM OF THOMAS BECKET.

▲ The tomb of Master Peter Seymour (Petrus de S. Mario), d. 1295.

by a mason with a poor grasp of Latin, confusingly reads 'Petrus de Sancta Maria'.

Floor Tiles

At around the time Peter Seymour died, decorative floor tiles were laid in the church. Various patterns may be seen, few (if any) in their original positions. Encaustic ('burnt in') tiles were made from two sorts of clay, red and white. The body of the tile was formed by packing a lump of red clay into a wooden frame. While the clay was still soft, a wooden mould carved with a pattern in relief was pressed into the upper surface, producing an indented matrix. Using a tool like a palette knife, a soft white clay was applied, filling the indents. When the white clay had dried somewhat, it was possible to pare off the excess with a knife, exposing the pattern. Scoops called 'keys' were dug in the underside, the upper surface was dipped in a lead glaze, and the tile was wood-fired in a single process.

▲ Fragments of the church's earliest known tile pavement (*c.*1300) used as hardcore in the 1860s.

The church's earliest tiles are so-called 'Wessex tiles' of around 1300. The most usual scheme comprised groups of four tiles with geometrical patterns, separated by a thin border of plain strips. Similar arrays of the same date occur in Winchester Cathedral's retrochoir. One of the most amusing is the 'mask' design, in which a human head, bearing a vague resemblance to the war-time 'Chad', peeks from one corner of the tile. When correctly assembled, these tiles form a roundel with four faces pointing inwards.

Another design was later used in the church, again in groups of four. These also formed a roundel, adorned with trefoils, fleurs-de-lys and, around the outside, the repeated words *Have Mynde* ('Remember!'), an exhortation to consider one's mortality. These tiles were made near Newbury in the mid-fifteenth century, and also occur in the

▲ An array of four geometric tiles, relaid in the 1860s but in their original configuration.

▲ FOUR 'MASK' TILES OF *c.*1300, IN AN ARRAY OF FOUR.

cathedral, where they were perhaps commissioned for Bishop Waynflete's chantry chapel. There are now no in-situ examples in St Cross Church, but one set, lacking its white slip inlay, is displayed on the north transept wall.

THE HOSPITAL IN THE FOURTEENTH CENTURY

By the early fourteenth century, despite the final severance of links with the Hospitallers, the governance of St Cross Hospital was somewhat shaky. Other hospitals were experiencing similar difficulties, and in 1311 Pope Clement V issued the bull *Quia Contingit* (named after its initial words), decreeing that the heads of hospitals should send annual inventories of the institutions' property to their diocesan bishops. This was evidently to stop the masters pocketing most of the income and providing only as little charitable benefaction as they could get away with. Almost immediately the master of St Cross, Robert Maidstone, was investigated by the new bishop, Henry Woodlock. Robert was an unashamed pluralist, with two livings and a canonry of Chichester Cathedral, but ill-doing was not proved, and he survived several attempts to deprive him of the mastership.

In 1321 Bishop Rigaud d'Assier, descendant of the feudal lords of the village of Assier in the Lot valley, appointed his kinsman Gerald d'Assier as his

agent. The following February Gerald conducted an enquiry into the 'defects of the houses of the master of St Cross'. The result is unknown. Subsequently another member of the family, Bertrand, became master. There is no evidence of financial irregularity, though an eyebrow might today be raised at keeping ecclesiastical offices in the family. But Bertrand's successor, Peter de Galiciano, a Spaniard and former rector of Horncastle (Lincs), was certainly unscrupulous. He was soon accused of squandering the hospital's income in the support of emigrants, 'suspected and foreign persons, who take flight to foreign parts'. The problem was temporarily solved by sequestrating the hospital's assets, but Master Peter persuaded Edward III to support his cause.

The next master was altogether a more significant figure: William of Edington, named after his native Wiltshire village. In 1331 William entered the service of the bishop of Winchester, Adam Orleton, who in 1335 appointed him master of St Cross. William occupied the post until 1345, when he succeeded Adam as bishop. He had allegedly previously been offered the archbishopric of Canterbury, which he refused, exclaiming 'though Canterbury be the higher rack, Winchester

▲ 'HAVE MYNDE' TILES: A MID-FIFTEENTH CENTURY TYPE MADE IN THE NEWBURY AREA.

◀ THE ALABASTER TOMB EFFIGY OF WILLIAM OF EDINGTON, MASTER OF ST CROSS (1335–45) THEN BISHOP OF WINCHESTER (1345–66).

is the richer manger'. By then William was Edward III's treasurer, a post that he held for twelve years before becoming the king's chancellor. Almost immediately after his consecration as bishop he began to rebuild the cathedral's west front, and later he started to refashion the cathedral nave. His interest in building projects began, however, during his mastership of the hospital.

When Edington became master the church's nave was little more than a building site. The side walls rose only just above main arcade level, and the nave had been temporarily roofed in thatch eighty years previously, to prevent deterioration of the incomplete masonry. An early fifteenth-century memorandum describes how Edington raised the side walls and built and glazed the clerestory windows. These have curvilinear tracery, typical

of the period, though the original glass has been replaced. The raising of the side walls also allowed the fine west window to be inserted. Edington actually created a more flamboyant west front than survives today, for there were 'two pinnacles at the west end of the church'. They must have been extensions of the stair turrets, culminating in pyramidal roofs. Finally, he roofed the nave in lead. Had he not been promoted bishop he would no doubt have vaulted the nave, but this was left to a later master.

THE LAYOUT OF THE MEDIEVAL HOSPITAL

From Edington's mastership comes also the first fragmentary documentary evidence which, combined with new archaeological findings, is gradually leading to a greater understanding of the layout of the hospital's domestic buildings in the centuries before Cardinal Beaufort's major reorganisation in the 1440s. Today the precincts are divided roughly equally into two rectangular areas aligned north-south. The western half comprises Beaufort's hospital buildings. At the north end is the outer court; between it and the church

◀ WILLIAM OF EDINGTON'S NAVE CLERESTORY AND WEST WINDOW. THE FLANKING PINNACLES THAT HE ADDED HAVE LONG GONE.

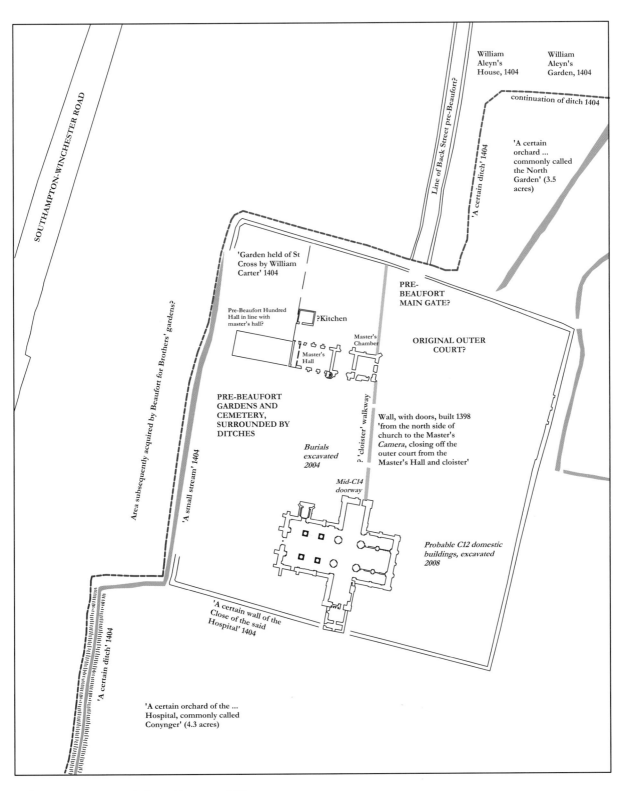

SOUTHAMPTON–WINCHESTER ROAD

William Aleyn's House, 1404

William Aleyn's Garden, 1404

Line of Back Street pre-Beaufort?

continuation of ditch 1404

'A certain ditch' 1404

'A certain orchard ... commonly called the North Garden' (3.5 acres)

'Garden held of St Cross by William Carter' 1404

PRE-BEAUFORT MAIN GATE?

Pre-Beaufort Hundred Hall in line with master's hall?

?Kitchen

Master's Chamber

ORIGINAL OUTER COURT?

Area subsequently acquired by Beaufort for Brothers' gardens?

Master's Hall

PRE-BEAUFORT GARDENS AND CEMETERY, SURROUNDED BY DITCHES

?'cloister' walkway

Wall, with doors, built 1398 'from the north side of church to the Master's *Camera*, closing off the outer court from the Master's Hall and cloister'

Burials excavated 2004

'A small stream' 1404

Mid-C14 doorway

Probable C12 domestic buildings, excavated 2008

'A certain wall of the Close of the said Hospital' 1404

'A certain ditch' 1404

'A certain orchard of the ... Hospital, commonly called Conynger' (4.3 acres)

▲ CONJECTURAL LAYOUT OF ST CROSS HOSPITAL IN 1401, BASED ON A CONTEMPORARY SURVEY.
THE RED LINE INDICATES THE BOUNDARY AT THAT TIME. © JOHN CROOK.

are the domestic buildings arranged around the quadrangle, including the Brethren's Hall. The eastern half is now an open space comprising the Master's Garden and Bowling Green.

It is becoming apparent that before Beaufort's time the distribution of residential buildings and open space was the other way around. The accommodation for the thirteen brothers of Henry of Blois's hospital, and for chaplains and other staff, was located in the eastern half of the precincts, but much of the western half was occupied by gardens and a cemetery. This more open area presumably also served as the 'public' access to the church via the north porch or, for ceremonial events, the west door. People would have enjoyed totally unrestricted movement between the two halves of the precincts until 1398, when Master John de Campeden built a wall separating the two areas, and even then his chronicler noted that it had doors in it. Forty years later, the central part of the western half of the precincts provided a clear site for Beaufort's Almshouse of Noble Poverty. Within a few decades, when his foundation failed, and the thirteen members of Henry of Blois's hospital moved into the accommodation originally intended for Beaufort's almsmen, the eastern half of the precincts became the area of lawns and gardens seen today. The definitive separation of the two halves of the precinct occurred *c*.1500 with the construction of the ambulatory.

The accommodation provided by Henry of Blois for the original thirteen poor brothers appears to have been on the site of the Bowling Green, east of the church. This was the secluded part of the hospital, the innermost court, linked to the church by the brothers' private cloister between the choir and south transept. North of the original lodgings was an outer court, the position of whose entrance gate may perhaps be inferred from the alignment of the main part of Back Street, the approach road from Winchester. As one comes down the street today, it veers to the right about a hundred yards from the hospital. This change in alignment probably dates from the fifteenth century, when the present gateway was established, but before then it may have run in a straight line to the early medieval entrance. The north side of the east end of the church, elaborately decorated for show, would have been visible to people coming down the street,

rising above the low domestic buildings.

The original position of one important building is uncertain. This is the hall where the local poor claimed their daily issue of provisions. The building in the present outer court called the Hundred Menne's Hall seems to date from the mid-fifteenth century, but a memorandum from around 1405 indicates that the earlier hall was located elsewhere. It states that William of Edington, master 1335–45, 'made the roof of the hall called *Hundredemenhalle* which now is divided into two halls: the hall for the master and his household, and the hall of the hundred men.' As we shall see, the master's hall (now the Brethren's Hall) was almost certainly built by William's nephew John in the 1360s, but he may have modified a much longer, earlier building that had been reroofed by his uncle. The clear implication of the 1405 memorandum, describing the layout known to its author, is that at that time the Hundred Menne's Hall formed a prolongation of the master's hall towards the west: it could not have extended eastwards, as this area was occupied by a gate-tower and the master's chamber.

The gardens and cemetery comprising the other half of the early medieval hospital, before Beaufort's reorganisation, are mentioned in various contemporary documents. In 1406, for example, 'the ditches that surround the cemetery and gardens' were cleaned out as part of John of Campeden's works. Spectacular evidence for the cemetery was discovered in 2004, when a rainwater soakaway was dug in the quadrangle. The excavation went through several archaeological layers: medieval tiles used as nineteenth-century hardcore, a flint surface (probably a fifteenth-century path), then greensand chippings deposited during late medieval building operations, but at the bottom many graves were discovered. The way successive graves cut through earlier ones was evidence of a long history of burials. People had probably been buried here since the hospital was founded, for the fill of the earliest graves included Caen stone chippings, the material from which the church was first built. But the skeletons were not of old men, as one might have expected, but a 'mixed population', including women and children, perhaps the wives and children of the medieval hospital's lay servants. St Cross had no parochial function until the early sixteenth century, and inhabitants of Sparkford would have been buried at the local parish church of St Faith. A cemetery would, however, have been needed for members of the wider hospital community, and it is plausible that they were interred locally.

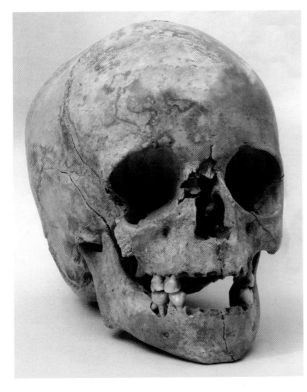

▲ THE SKULL OF A CHILD, DISCOVERED DURING THE EXCAVATION OF A SOAKAWAY.

Edington's successors, Raymond de Pelegrini and Richard Lusteshall (who simply exchanged posts with Master Raymond), made little impact on the hospital. Then in April 1349 the bishop appointed his nephew John of Edington as master of St Cross and rector of Cheriton; two years later the bishop added the archdeaconry of Surrey to John's fat portfolio. Needless to say, the appointment to St Cross later led to a charge of nepotism: Edington's successor, William of Wykeham, referred to 'certain bishops of Winchester who had appointed their nephews', but Edington was probably within his rights. Although John of Edington lacked the fine moral qualities of his uncle, his appointment had one successful consequence: it was almost certainly he who constructed, albeit for his own use, the hall now known as the 'Brethren's Hall' which is the most spectacular of the domestic buildings of St Cross Hospital.

THE BEGINNINGS OF THE BRETHREN'S HALL

It is sometimes supposed that the Brethren's Hall and the Beaufort Tower were built by Cardinal Beaufort in the 1440s, when he founded the Almshouse of Noble Poverty. The error is pardonable: the interior of the hall and the exterior of the tower bear an ostentatious display of the bishop's coat of arms. In fact the hall was built in the fourteenth century as the master's hall, but was

▶ THE FOURTEENTH-CENTURY WINDOWS OF THE BRETHREN'S HALL. THE ONE ON THE RIGHT WAS MOVED WESTWARDS AT THE END OF THE CENTURY TO ACCOMMODATE THE OCTAGONAL STAIR TURRET.

taken over by Beaufort to serve as a common hall for his new brethren.

The first clue to the date of the hall is the style of its windows. These have a cross-shaped array of four main lights separated by a horizontal transom and a vertical mullion. The upper lights have two-centred arches at the top, with cinquefoil cusping. At the head of the whole window, also contained within a two-centred arch, is tracery of a very characteristic form. In the middle is an elongated quatrefoil, flanked by short vertical elements that are very slightly curved. It is above all this tracery design that is so typical of the third quarter of the fourteenth century, and which immediately indicates that the hall was built long before the time of Cardinal Beaufort.

Viewed from outside, the windows seem rather high up, and this is because the hall is raised well above external ground level on cellarage, whose present entrance is a later doorway at the foot of the corner of the Beaufort Tower. Originally the basement comprised two slightly pointed tunnel vaults running the entire length of the building and lit by low side windows. Only one window now survives on the north side. During Beaufort's refurbishment slightly more than half of the original basement was replaced by an elegantly vaulted beer cellar, truncating the earlier tunnels.

The main entrance to the hall is at the top of a flight of steps within a porch. A proud display of Beaufort's arms in the keystone of the vault leaves no doubt that the porch was added by the cardinal when he adapted the hall in the 1440s.

Originally there must have been just an external stair, and the right-hand wall of the porch replaced a buttress similar to the others on this side of the hall. The main doorway, however, is a primary feature of the building, and its style allows us to date the hall with some certainty. The doorway is typical of developed Perpendicular architecture, the quintessentially English building style that flourished after the Black Death of 1348–9. Its mouldings are a smaller-scale, gracile version of those employed by Bishop William of Edington for two new side doors, now blocked, at the west end of his cathedral aisles, dating from the early 1360s.

The most reliable features for dating purposes, however, are the hood-mould stops of the south door, featuring a king and a queen. The king must be Edward III in middle age (he was born in 1312); the queen, his consort, Philippa of Hainault. She died in 1369, aged fifty-five, and it is unlikely that she would have been represented posthumously. Unless they are stylistically very archaic, the carvings cannot date from the time of Edward III's successor, Richard II, who ascended the throne aged ten in 1377 and did not marry until 1382. Thus a date in the 1360s seems likely, and this is supported by a documentary reference to building works being undertaken by John of Edington towards the end of his mastership. An entry in William of Wykeham's episcopal register notes that John abused his position as rector of Farnham to appropriate a large number of building stones intended for works at the parish church there, some of which he transported to St Cross. This suggests that John was involved

◀ THE FOURTEENTH-CENTURY BASEMENT, COMPRISING TWO PARALLEL TUNNEL-VAULTS OF POINTED PROFILE, PROBABLY ORIGINALLY CONTINUING THROUGHOUT THE FULL LENGTH OF THE HALL ABOVE.

▲ Fourteenth-century door to the hall, enclosed within Cardinal Beaufort's new porch of the 1440s.

in some private building initiative at the hospital. What he created was akin to a medieval manor house with hall and chamber. As already noted, he may have taken over part of the fabric of an earlier range of buildings that had been reroofed during the mastership of his uncle William, separating and rebuilding the east end to form his own hall, but leaving the Hundred Menne's Hall at the west end.

The entrance doorway leads into a cross-passage, separated from the body of the hall by a wooden screen. The passage is certainly a primary feature, and explains why the westernmost bay of the four-bay hall is shorter than the others. Such cross-passages are typical of medieval halls: they were invariably located at the 'low' end of the hall, the other being the 'high' end, where the master sat in state. The configuration is still to be found in Oxford or Cambridge dining halls, with their 'high table' raised on a dais.

The original screen defining the cross-passage at the low end consisted of a pair of simple wooden wing walls extending from the sides of the hall, with a free-standing screen in the middle. The central portion has been replaced, and arched doorways fill the gaps, but the original wings survive as the outer ends of the present screen. The passage would not have had a ceiling; the gallery above it was a much later feature. Often in medieval

▲ Royal heads forming the stops to the hood-mould of the hall's main door. They are thought to represent Edward III and Queen Philippa of Hainault and were later regrettably defaced, probably during the Commonwealth.

halls there were doors in the end wall, leading to pantry, buttery, and a detached kitchen, but there are no signs of this having been the case at St Cross. As we have seen, it is possible that the Hundred Menne's Hall continued the line of the master's hall towards the west, and this would have required placing the service buildings in a different location from usual. The kitchen, probably detached because of the fire risk, seems to have stood north of the hall, linked to it by a covered way of some sort. Indeed, the door at the north end of the passage opens inwards, showing that this doorway led into the open. This door is more complete than the south, entrance door, which has been aggressively modified over the centuries.

The body of the hall now has three windows on the south side and two on the north. It is likely that there was a third window on the north side, before the north wing containing the kitchen was added in the late 1440s; in this bay there is now a mid-fifteenth century doorway opening into the 'bread room'. The wall here has been much altered, including the removal of a buttress. The pair of windows at the east end are more elaborate than the others, having window-seats, and the south-east window is not in its original position.

The hall in its fourteenth-century form was presumably heated by a central hearth, and smoke probably escaped through a louvre above it. The complete replacement of the roof in the 1440s would have obliterated all evidence of a louvre. After the cardinal's refurbishment warmth was probably provided by charcoal braziers, producing less smoke than burning logs. In the later seventeenth century the brothers still enjoyed 'a fire of charcoal in the common hall' on the eve of certain major church feasts, and this heating system probably went back to medieval times.

The Administration in Difficulties

John of Edington's hall was added for his own benefit rather than for the good of the hospital, and his mastership marked the beginning of a period when Bishop Henry's charitable intentions were sorely challenged. The hall was probably scarcely complete when in 1366–70 a rapid succession of

◀ THE BRETHREN'S HALL IN THE EARLY NINETEENTH CENTURY. THE CROSS-PASSAGE IS BEHIND THE WOODEN SCREEN AT THE END, BENEATH THE LATER GALLERY.

▶ Tomb effigy of Bishop William of Wykeham, Winchester Cathedral.

leadership changes occurred: John exchanged the mastership with William Stowell, who soon passed it to Richard of Lyntesford. Within two years, in August 1370, Lyntesford had exchanged with the archdeacon of Ripon, Roger de Cloune. Such exchanges were frequent amongst clergymen in the fourteenth century, allowing them to obtain what they considered better posts without the chore of episcopal presentation.

Lyntesford took up the post in March 1368, when Winchester was about to welcome a new bishop, William of Wykeham. Rebuilder of the nave of Winchester Cathedral, founder of New College Oxford and Winchester College, Wykeham was one of the richest and most influential people in the land. He immediately took a close look at the hospital founded by his Anglo-Norman predecessor. Perhaps suspecting that some unscrupulous dealings had occurred during all these exchanges of mastership, he wrote to Stowell, emphasising that as bishop it was his duty to ensure that the hospital's material possessions were not sold off to the advantage of others (i.e. the master), and warning that he would not turn a blind eye towards abuses. He demanded a full inventory and condition survey of the hospital's chattels: the goods, corn, animals, utensils, tools, and other similar items that Stowell had passed on to Lyntesford. Wykeham then pursued his enquiry back nearly twenty years, appointing an official

to find out what goods (including 'silver vessels, and ornaments') John of Edington had received from Master Lusteshall in 1349. The chase was on, and in July 1370 Wykeham commissioned two officials to visit the hospital and examine the four successive masters: Edington, Stowell, Lyntesford, and de Cloune.

At the basis of Wykeham's enquiry was an important question: was the mastership of St Cross, for which the bishops of Winchester were responsible, an ecclesiastical benefice without the 'care of souls', or was the institution a hospital as defined by Pope Clement V in his bull *Quia Contingit*? Were it possible to prove that the post was a sinecure benefice, the masters could argue that, provided they maintained the poor in accordance with the founder's instructions, they were entitled to the surplus revenue, perhaps even to the hospital's possessions.

It must have been fairly clear to the four successive masters that this was unlikely to be Wykeham's understanding, and Roger de Cloune made a pre-emptive strike, accusing his three predecessors of deliberately running down the hospital to their own advantage. Within a year or two Lyntesford and Stowell had made their declarations of submission, agreeing that St Cross was indeed a hospital as defined by the pope, accepting that all its goods were intended to sustain the poor rather than belonging to the master, and

▲ The Hospital of St Cross from the north-east in 1783.

yielding to the bishop's decision. Having gained the moral high ground, Stowell and Lyntesford then turned the tables on de Cloune, accusing him of squandering the hospital's resources, to such an extent that 'even the dwelling houses and other places which their predecessors had so generously built had collapsed to the ground through his negligence'; a desperate attempt to show that the losses had occurred since de Cloune's appointment scarcely two years previously. Now, in January 1373, it was de Cloune's turn to face the charges. Even so, the guilt of all four successive masters was evidently suspected, and the following month Wykeham commissioned four senior churchmen to pronounce sentence upon them.

An enquiry revealed that de Cloune had indeed been guilty of 'dilapidations' during his mastership, even during Wykeham's inquisition. In March 1373 the master was summoned to answer the charges before eight local laymen in the bishop's consistory court. Meanwhile de Cloune had written to the highest authority, the pope, asking whether the conditions of *Quia Contingit* applied in this case. Gregory XI replied from Avignon: de Cloune had no right to alienate the hospital's property. The pope agreed with Wykeham that de Cloune's appeal was simply an attempt at playing for time. By July the hospital's income (the 'temporals') had been confiscated from de Cloune, and soon he was summoned to appear before the bishop in Esher parish church to answer a charge of having stopped the daily provision of food to the hundred men.

The case against de Cloune rumbled on for another year. He refused to accept the judgements against him, broke the terms of the sequestration of the hospital's assets, and encouraged his deputy William of Castleford to continue in the despoliation. But by December 1373 things were

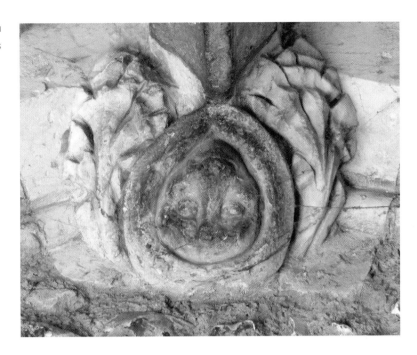

▶ A CORBEL IN THE FORM OF AN INVERTED HEAD IN THE GATE PASSAGE BENEATH BEAUFORT'S TOWER IS OFTEN CLAIMED TO REPRESENT MASTER ROGER DE CLOUNE, TURNED UPSIDE DOWN AS A PUNISHMENT.

drawing to a close, and Thomas of Baketon, a Lincolnshire canon charged with hearing the case against the four recalcitrant masters, issued his judgement. St Cross was indeed a hospital within the meaning of *Quia Contingit*, and its successive masters were responsible for producing an annual audit. De Cloune got off lightly: he was compelled to submit an inventory, and was ordered to pay the bishop's legal costs.

Wykeham's inquisition had one fortunate side-effect: it has left much information about life in the hospital in the fourteenth century. It must have been a lively place, the thirteen brethren being outnumbered by a choir of twenty clerks and singing boys, four chaplains, a cook, three bakers, three brewers, and sundry other servants. The choristers were recruited from the local poor. Each day they were given a dish of food, a loaf of bread, and a quart of small beer; they also received a rudimentary education. The brethren were adequately fed, with three dishes for their mid-day dinner: bread and milk, meat or fish, and a 'dish of the day', together with a generous measure of beer and sufficient bread. Supper was a single dish. On church feast days the meat was of better quality and the beer ration was quadrupled; on these occasions the hundred poor also enjoyed increased rations. The latter group included thirteen poor scholars, sent down the road daily by the master of the city grammar school.

For the next eight years de Cloune remained titular master (though technically deprived of the post in December 1374 and living abroad), but Wykeham's kinsman Nicholas Wykeham, the archdeacon of Winchester, was appointed sequestrator, managing the hospital until de Cloune's death. He fulfilled all the functions of a master, though he was never actually appointed to this post. Then, in 1383, one of the hospital's best-loved masters took office, as described in the next chapter.

Chapter 4

JOHN DE CAMPEDEN
1383–1410

In February 1383 John de Campeden, rector of Cheriton and archdeacon of Surrey, became master. He is still remembered as one of St Cross's most generous benefactors. Mindful of the difficulties with previous masters, Bishop William of Wykeham took no chances, and the charter of appointment emphasised that Campeden should conform with Pope Clement's bull *Quia Contingit*. An inventory of the hospital's possessions

was accordingly drawn up. The steward, Henry Derneford, dutifully counted the livestock: there were eleven horses, four cows, three calves, a boar, two sows, twenty pigs, twenty piglets, and four capons. He listed the contents of various buildings: the hall, pantry, brewhouse, kitchen, cart-shed, granary, and the church vestry where, amongst many other things, Henry counted twenty-one chasubles and twenty-seven albs, including four for boys.

JOHN DE CAMPEDEN'S ARCHITECTURAL LEGACY

John de Campeden's extensive works on the church are recorded in unusual detail in a contemporary text called the *St Cross Register*. In 1383–5 the choir roof, in a state of collapse, was renewed. Scars on the sides of the tower show that the transepts were also reroofed at this time, slightly lower than before. Glazed windows were inserted into the tower walls, just above the four new abutting roofs. The pattern of the window tracery is a rather more utilitarian version of that previously used in the Brethren's Hall. Above the windows is a string course, part of a well integrated design. Originally there was to have been an external arcade of

◀ A PORTRAIT OF MASTER JOHN DE CAMPEDEN FROM HIS MEMORIAL BRASS.

unglazed openings, five on each face of the tower, in front of an enclosed passage running around the tower between the thin outer wall and a thicker inner one, for at this level there is a double skin of masonry supported on the tall arches visible from below within the crossing tower. The external arcade would have given plenty of borrowed light to the bell-chamber via splayed windows in the inner wall. There are just four of these inner openings, one at the centre of each face, with cinquefoil heads. The lack of holes for iron bars (*ferramenta*) suggests that they were never glazed (though grooves show this was the initial intention), so most of the twenty exterior arches were probably blocked almost as soon as they were completed. Only the central openings of each face remained open, opposite the inner windows, and Y-tracery was crudely inserted into these four outer windows, which were then glazed.

The *Register* mentions the belfry ceiling (*celura*), and this is what one sees inside the crossing from below. It is a colourful affair, a plausible nineteenth-century repainting of woodwork that certainly would have originally been brightly painted. The floor is supported on short shafts held up by carved stone head corbels, in wonderful condition in this protected environment and with some of their original polychrome. The male heads have the forked beard that became so fashionable in Richard II's reign, and their grotesque character prefigures some of the vault bosses of Winchester Cathedral's nave, built two decades later.

▲ A GROTESQUE CORBEL SUPPORTING THE BELFRY CEILING IN THE NORTH-EAST CORNER OF THE TOWER.

◀ THE NORTH FACE OF THE TOWER. THE ROOF SLOPE HAS CLEARLY BEEN LOWERED SLIGHTLY. THE LARGE LOWER WINDOW IS ONE OF EIGHT INSERTED BY JOHN DE CAMPEDEN TO ALLOW LIGHT TO ENTER THE SPACE BELOW THE TOWER CEILING WITHIN. HIGHER UP, FIVE OPENINGS ON EACH FACE WERE ORIGINALLY INTENDED TO FORM AN OPEN ARCADE LIGHTING THE BELL-CHAMBER'S FOUR INNER WINDOWS.

At the same time Campeden also altered the lighting of the chancel. The triforium openings were originally intended simply to light the roof spaces from within. Master John reversed things, lowering the roofs over the aisles and glazing the sixteen outer triforium openings so that light could flood in from eight new windows on each side. What must have been a rather dark and gloomy choir was transformed. These architectural works to the choir were followed by new fittings: stalls, clergy seating, and benches were introduced, and the reredos received a wall painting. On 8 December 1385 a new high altar was set up; four months later, on 28 April, it was consecrated in honour of the Holy Cross. It is described as being of alabaster, but its top slab or *mensa* appears to have been of Purbeck marble and was discovered in 1861 built into the choir's east wall. It was incorporated into the present high altar in 1929–30.

One might have expected the high altar to have been consecrated by Wykeham himself, but the *Register* is ambiguous on this point, stating only that the altar was consecrated in his nineteenth year as bishop. It does, however, say that on the same day his suffragan, Thomas Ashenden, consecrated an altar to St Katherine, so perhaps it was tacitly understood that the diocesan bishop would have consecrated the high altar. Certainly Wykeham was in Hampshire at the time, signing documents at Bishop's Waltham two days later. During the next three years other altars were consecrated, presumably marking the end of Campeden's major building works at the east end of the church. On 3 April 1387 four brothers moved a rood (a crucifix with statues of SS. Mary and John) into St John's chapel. It had previously stood in a *solarium* on the north side of the nave, presumably the chamber over the porch. On 17 March 1388, Ashenden consecrated an altar 'next to the sacristy', dedicated to SS. Ursula and Sitha, the Thousand Virgins, and St Stephen. Also mentioned is an altar dedicated to the Virgin Mary and St Thomas of Canterbury, perhaps a rededication of the one within the painted niche in the south transept.

Campeden also undertook remedial works in the choir, strengthening the central piers between the paired arches on either side. Their design had already been modified when they were first built because the original masonry was not strong enough to take the weight. In 1387–8 John de Campeden modified them again, 'making the two stone columns in the chancel'. In fact what he did was to encase the Purbeck pillars in stone to an octagonal form. The fourteenth-century casing was removed by the architect William Butterfield in the 1860s, and something closer to the twelfth-century design was reinstated, though with square central piers rather than the circular ones used by the Romanesque master masons.

Various other works are recorded, amongst the most significant being the repaving of the church, 'including its chancel and aisles', in 1389–90. Encaustic tiles were again used, many of which have survived. The designs are identical to those

◀ 'CASTLE' TILES NEAR THE FONT.

laid at the cathedral in the 1390s and at Winchester College, where they are mentioned in the college's accounts. Thus we know that the supplier was 'William the Tiler', of Otterbourne. Most of his designs were intended to be grouped in fours, and in the nineteenth century Butterfield reassembled some of the original designs in the aisles of the church. He also replicated several of the medieval designs in the new tiles made by Minton to pave the nave and chancel.

One of the most interesting medieval tile patterns features a castle. There is a group of these near the font, and it can be seen that the design looks damaged: one of the crenellations at the top of the tower is missing. This was a result of the way such tiles were made. Evidently at some stage part of the fiddly crenellated detail of the wooden mould broke off. There are examples of the complete pattern in the south-east retrochoir chapel in Winchester Cathedral, but by the time Bishop Wykeham built his chantry chapel in the nave *c.*1400 the 'castle' tiles used there showed the defect.

John de Campeden also initiated work on the nave vault. Fifty years previously William of Edington had completed the nave's main elevations, with their elegant clerestory windows, and had roofed the nave throughout its length. The open timber roof would have been visible from below.

▲ JOHN DE CAMPEDEN'S *ARMA CHRISTI* BADGE ADORNS A KEYSTONE OF THE NAVE VAULT WHICH HE BUILT.

An additional note in the *Register*, whose main entries ended in 1406–7, mentions Campeden's provision of money for the 'vault of the church, in part', suggesting that this had only just begun. His benefaction is commemorated by the main vault bosses depicting his personal badge, the so-called *'Arma Christi'*, a semi-heraldic representation of the instruments used for Jesus's Passion, including the 'pillar of the flagellation', and the nails, spear, and pincers of the Crucifixion. They also feature on his fine memorial brass, relocated in the chancel. The nave vault's other heraldic bosses include the arms of William of Wykeham, who appointed Campeden, and Cardinal Beaufort, in whose episcopate the vault was begun and completed.

Campeden's works were not restricted to the church. According to the *Register*, in 1390 he built 'eleven rooms with a chapel' for the thirteen brothers. It has already been suggested that Bishop Henry's original accommodation comprised the usual arrangement of a single hall with a chapel at the east end; by the late fourteenth century the brothers evidently enjoyed individual rooms. The *capella* of the *Register* was distinct from the church (*ecclesia*), and was presumably, like its predecessor, attached to the building containing the brothers' chambers. Then in around 1398 Master John built a stone wall with doors in it, running 'from the north side of the church as far as the master's chamber ... separating the outer court from the master's hall and the cloister'. There can be no doubt that the master's hall was the present brethren's hall built in the 1360s, which indicates that this wall ran northwards, still represented by the wall between the north-east corner of the transept and the porter's lodge. As we have seen, this formed a major boundary between two halves of the precincts, and Campeden's intention was presumably to delineate the master's enclave more strictly, though the provision of door *'valvas'* shows a concern to maintain access between the brothers' quarters to the east and the gardens and cemetery to the west. The 'cloister' mentioned in the document is harder to interpret, but the term could be used for a simple covered passage in the middle ages, and it possible that it refers to a predecessor to the present ambulatory, perhaps a simple pentice roof against the wall, allowing the master to walk from his chamber to the church under shelter.

Also recorded is the creation in 1393 of two 'windows called Standisshes' in the master's 'first chamber', for the convenience of Thomas, Earl of Kent, resident for the parliament assembled in Winchester that year. These were probably tall windows with window-seats, like those flanking the dais in the hall. In the same year a chimney-piece was constructed in the middle of the master's chamber. In 1406–7 Campeden provided 4,000 'pavyngtiles' for the 'hall' (*aula*): if these were the typical six-inch tiles of the period, the number would indeed fit the Brethren's Hall; the present larger tiles are presumably later replacements.

THE GATE-TOWER

Other works, perhaps carried out at the very end of John de Campeden's mastership appear to have gone almost unrecorded. The ostentatious display of Cardinal Beaufort's heraldry on the north side of the gate-tower named after him has blinded most observers to the fact that Campeden's own Passion badges flank the south arch of the same tower.

▲ ONE OF TWO HOOD-MOULD STOPS SURVIVING FROM THE FIRST GATE-TOWER, FEATURING JOHN DE CAMPEDEN'S *ARMA CHRISTI* BADGE: THE PINCERS, PILLAR OF THE FLAGELLATION, AND SCOURGES.

They provide an initial clue to a new discovery: the Beaufort Tower was not, as has previously been assumed, erected on an open space at the east end of what is now the Brethren's Hall in one single building operation of the 1440s, but incorporated elements of an earlier tower. There was thus an intermediate phase of building works between the fourteenth-century hall and the mid-fifteenth century 'Beaufort Tower'.

The main evidence for this is the constructional detail of the octagonal stair turret at the south-west corner of the main gate-tower. Externally, the lowest part of the turret, including its small doorway, is built of 'Green Ventnor' sandstone from the Upper Greensand quarries on the Isle of Wight. It has not weathered well, and several blocks were replaced in Caen stone in the nineteenth century, but otherwise greensand occurs consistently up to just over four metres above the ground. At this level is a narrower course of masonry, and thereafter smaller blocks of Caen stone are used. The transition is obvious if one looks at the tower from a distance, where a distinct change in colour from greenish to white may be seen. The half-buttress attached to the turret corresponds to a true buttress on the right-hand side of the tower's main arch, and in both of these a similar change in stone type is found, though there has been much modern replacement.

That the change in stone type does not simply reflect a change of building supply is evident as soon as one enters the stair turret. Looking up the spiral stair, one has the disquieting impression of being in a stone tube that has split down the middle and been repaired on one side. The earlier phase is manifested by large greensand blocks in a wide vertical band on the south side (the inner face of the turret's external wall), a style of masonry that continues up to about four metres above ground level. The second phase, forming the north side of the interior masonry of the turret and thus integral with the main body of the Beaufort Tower, consists of well-cut Caen stone blocks, much smaller than the greensand ones. The disjunction between the two phases is dramatic, and the horizontal courses of these two stone types do not match up, a clear indication of different constructional phases. Furthermore, the actual spiral stair has clearly been rebuilt, for its treads simply abut the earlier

◀ TWO PHASES OF MASONRY WITHIN THE STAIR TURRET, MANIFESTED BY AN OBVIOUS VERTICAL DISJUNCTION AND LACK OF COURSING.

The spiral stair in the turret was evidently intended to give access to an upper-storey room east of the hall. Twenty-one steps up, at the point where the stair winds closest to the corner of the hall, there is a blocked doorway, demonstrably of the turret's first phase (the left-hand jamb courses with the big greensand blocks). This doorway was retained when the turret was rebuilt. It led obliquely through the south wall of the hall and emerged quite near the inner corner. The shadowy outline of its four-centred arch is still discernible in the wall next to the shifted window. Obviously this high-level doorway was at the top of a stair. The present

masonry rather than being integral with it, the way such stairs were normally built. The treads are of greensand, presumably reused when the stair was reconstructed, and in that reconstruction the treads and the masonry of the turret's walls were properly bonded.

The first phase comprised much more than just the stair turret. As now, it formed the corner of a gate-tower, whose ground plan was probably identical to that of the present tower, including a gate passage with arches at either end (the north arch being slightly narrower than the south). So 'Beaufort's Tower' seems to be a reconstruction of an earlier gate-tower that either failed structurally or perhaps was never completed.

One might suppose that the earlier gate-tower would be contemporary with the fourteenth-century hall, but the structural evidence disproves this. The stair turret actually intrudes into the south-east corner of the hall, and at lower level one can see that the masonry of the two buildings is not coursed together as it would have been had they been contemporary. Furthermore, in order to accommodate the turret, the hall's south-east window has been shifted westwards, so it is incongruously close to the next buttress. This operation required rebuilding part of the side wall of the hall, between the window and the tower, and here the masonry does 'bond' together as one would expect if moving the window and building the turret took place simultaneously. Inside the building certain misalignments of the window's masonry, and joints that are wider than those of the other windows, confirm that it has been rebuilt in its new position.

▲ SOUTH SIDE OF THE BEAUFORT TOWER. A SLIGHT CHANGE IN THE COLOUR AND TEXTURE OF THE MASONRY OF THE STAIR TURRET INDICATES THE JUNCTION BETWEEN THE FIRST AND SECOND GATE-TOWERS.

stone stair, cutting across the window, is an early sixteenth-century modification, but the original one probably consisted of about nine steps, perhaps of timber, against the end wall of the hall. It would have intruded into the dais by only about seven feet.

So we have evidence of how the master got from the high end of the hall into his first-floor chamber over the gate passage, an arrangement retained when Beaufort rebuilt the gate-tower. On retiring the master would have walked up the short flight of steps, through the upper doorway in the corner of the hall, then up nine more steps within the turret to another doorway leading into the chamber over the gate. Beaufort's remodelled version of this second doorway is still in place. It seems a circuitous route, but Beaufort had inherited a pre-existing access arrangement that could not easily be modified. Perhaps it was in Beaufort's time that additional security was provided by a metal gate blocking the spiral stair just below the first doorway. Its fittings are still in place.

Who then was responsible for the first gate-tower? That great building master, John de Campeden is the most likely candidate, for his badge occurs in the end-stops either side of the tower's great south arch. This is crucial evidence, for the archaeological and stylistic details are of little help for determining the date of the first gate-tower. Greensand had already been employed for the buttresses of the hall, and was favoured in the 1390s for the buildings of Winchester College.

Beaufort used both greensand and Caen stone, the latter especially for more detailed work, such as his undercroft and the doors within his tower. The 'four-centred' (Tudor arch) profile of the little doorway at the foot of the stair turret was common from the later fourteenth century, and was used by Campeden in his entrance to the church belfry, and the fact that the arch is four-centred is another indication that the turret post-dates the hall. On the other hand, the profile of this doorway seems altogether clumsier than Beaufort's doors of the 1440s, which are characterised by simplicity, their only adornment being a broach stop just above ground level. The outside head stops of the weather mould over the turret doorway are too weathered to be of much use for dating purposes.

There is, unfortunately, no good documentary evidence to confirm that John de Campeden was responsible for the first gate-tower, as suggested here. As already observed, the entries in the *St Cross Register* cease in around 1407, three years before Campeden's death. However, the main purpose of the *Register* was to provide information about things that the master had done for the general good of the hospital, not for himself. The fact he signed his work with his personal badge is as good a proof of his involvement as any conveniently surviving document.

John de Campeden lies in the chancel of his church. His fine brass was reset by Butterfield, but probably in the original position. In 1838 the author Robert Mudie had observed that the monument was subject to a strange phenomenon: if the wind rose outside, the brass would emit a whistling sound. It must have been an eerie experience.

◀ A small commemorative tile with John de Campeden's initials and the date 1410 in early Arabic numerals, reset in the nave by Butterfield.

Chapter 5

CARDINAL BEAUFORT'S NEW FOUNDATION 1439–1447

Apart from the church, the Brethren's Hall, and part of the stair turret of the gate-tower, almost all of the hospital's extant domestic buildings were constructed in the mid-fifteenth century by Cardinal Henry Beaufort. In several respects, his influence on the hospital echoes that of Henry of Blois three hundred years earlier. Both were royal siblings, both were bishops of Winchester, and both were amongst the most powerful men in the kingdom.

▲ THE SEVENTEENTH-CENTURY TOMB EFFIGY OF CARDINAL BEAUFORT IN WINCHESTER CATHEDRAL. THE MEDIEVAL ORIGINAL WAS DESTROYED DURING THE COMMONWEALTH.

Henry Beaufort was born around 1375, one of the children of John of Gaunt and Katherine Swinford. They were not yet married, and later Henry, a bastard, had to be legitimised. Gaunt's first wife was Blanche of Lancaster (d. 1368), whose only surviving son was Henry Bolingbroke, the future Henry IV. So Beaufort and the king were half-brothers, and it was through Henry IV's influence that Beaufort became chancellor in 1403 and bishop of Winchester the following year, in succession to William of Wykeham. Beaufort's influence continued under Henry V, and at the height of his career he was the richest prelate in the land, able to lend the king a huge sum of money to continue the French campaign after Agincourt. His political fortunes changed with the accession of the boy king Henry VI and the start of a long-running feud with Humphrey, Duke of Gloucester. Nevertheless the 'Rich Cardinal' (he obtained the cardinal's hat in 1417 thanks to his support of Pope Martin V) remained to the end his life a powerful and influential statesman, though regarded by many as ambitious and unscrupulous.

THE ALMSHOUSE OF NOBLE POVERTY

By the late 1430s Beaufort was beginning to withdraw from public affairs, and it was in this final period of his life that he resolved to found an 'Almshouse of Noble Poverty', to accommodate thirty-five brethren and three sisters. The brethren were intended to be either men of aristocratic birth who had fallen on hard times or members of Beaufort's own household. They were not necessarily as ancient or decrepit as the 'impotent' individuals of the original hospital, and there is evidence that some of them played an active role

▲ An eighteenth-century aerial view of the hospital by William Cave, showing the Beaufort Tower and the Brethren's Hall, with the quadrangle beyond. The south range, adjoining the church, was demolished in 1789.

in the new foundation's affairs, riding around the country on hospital business.

The status of the 'sisters' is less clear. It is often assumed that they were either nuns, brought in to minister to the brethren's needs, or 'sisters' in the way the term is still used to denote a nurse. They certainly lived in common in their own 'house', had their own small 'hall', and their duties included 'washing the brethren's clothes'. Yet they received exactly the same annual stipend as the brothers (28s 8d plus 2d a day for 'table money'), were provided with identical dark red gowns, and as far as was possible at that time seem to have enjoyed equal rights. They seem, in short, to have been seculars rather than religious, so to refer to them as nuns is probably incorrect.

The intention was that both Henry of Blois's original establishment and Beaufort's new foundation should run in parallel, using the same church, and under the same master, Thomas

Forest, who had held the post since 1426. Bishop Henry's thirteen poor men would continue to live in their existing rooms, east of the church. For the noble newcomers Beaufort planned extensive new accommodation in the comparatively empty western half of the precincts; the two foundations would literally co-exist side by side.

In 1439 Beaufort began to purchase land in order to provide financial support for the intended foundation. Royal permission to take over ('alienate') these manors and lordships was granted in 1443, and in February 1446 the formal statute of the new foundation was issued. By Beaufort's death in 1447 his great quadrangle and the north kitchen wing were nearly finished. Three years later the new foundation was complete, with a total of two priests, thirty-five brethren, and three sisters.

It was in the spacious garden and cemetery area that Cardinal Beaufort set out the great quadrangle that so impresses visitors as they pass through the tower that bears his name. Two sides were determined by existing structures: on the north, John of Edington's hall and the adjacent gate-tower and master's lodgings; and on the east, the boundary wall that de Campeden had created *c.*1398, running between the corner of the church's north transept and the master's lodgings on the east side of the first gate-tower. This wall would serve as the boundary between the old and new foundations. Beaufort rebuilt the tower (retaining part of the earlier structure), and reconstructed the master's lodgings next to it. He enclosed the area to the south and west with a range that lay corner to corner with the church's west front: it ran first westwards, then returned northwards, and finally eastwards to join the west end of the hall. This produced a quadrangle that was not square like a monastic cloister but elongated to north and south. There were thirty-six apartments (thirty-five and a spare), not counting the two corners at the ends of the long sides; perhaps these

housed the chaplains. It is not known where the sisters' house stood. Beaufort appears to have enlarged the precincts slightly towards the west, adding the long north-south strip of land now occupied by the brothers' gardens; previously the hospital boundary had stepped in at the south end of this area as described in the 1401 survey (see the plan on p. 29).

Before any above-ground work could begin, Beaufort or his architect gave careful thought to the important question of sanitation. Henry of Blois's hospital probably had a sanitary block like a monastic rere-dorter, flushed by a watercourse diverted from the Itchen; it perhaps survives as the ditch that crosses the meadow north-east of the hospital and flows just outside the precinct wall. But Beaufort created a masonry-lined watercourse known as the 'Lockburn' (a corruption of *l'orte bourne*, 'dirty stream'), which would run around the periphery of the quadrangle. Its feeder stream was not the Itchen, but the Mill Stream,

▲ Beaufort's quadrangle from the south. The present view into the quadrangle was created when the south range was demolished in 1789.

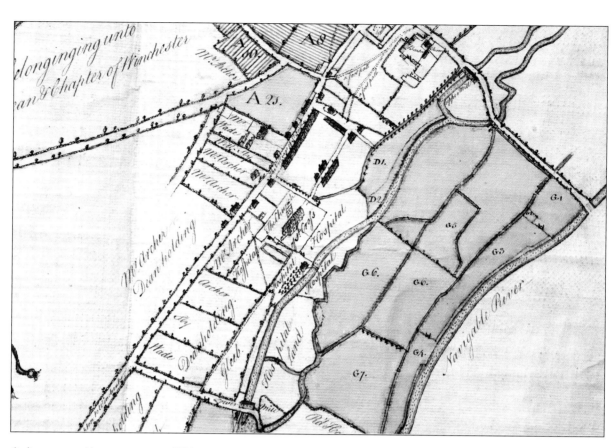

▲ A plan of the Hospital grounds c.1750 by the surveyor John Godson shows (top) the feeder stream of the drain called the 'Lockburn', which branches off the City Mill Stream just north of the former Barton (Upper) Mill. The wider channel depicted is the feeder stream to St Cross Mill, whose straight course contrasts with the zig-zag original course of the Itchen.

a watercourse that had doubled as an open sewer since Anglo-Saxon times. It still gathers the waters of the Brooks within Winchester's city walls but previously also served as the drain of the cathedral priory and Winchester College. The stream flows due south from College Mill to the site of Barton Mill in Garnier Road, its straight course contrasting with the meandering Itchen in the adjacent water meadows, and the Lockburn branches off from the Mill Stream just above Barton Mill.

Beaufort's notion of the needs of impoverished gentlefolk was very different from that of his twelfth-century predecessor. Each of his thirty-five brothers was to have a separate apartment, and the layout of the surviving parts of his domestic accommodation reflects this. It was set out on the lines of an Oxbridge college. Unlike the bishops that came before and after him, Beaufort did not found a college at Oxford, and St Cross was perhaps a kind of substitute. The basic unit of an Oxford college is the 'staircase'; likewise at St Cross, the accommodation consists of suites of rooms grouped

▶ The brothers' quarters are grouped in fours.

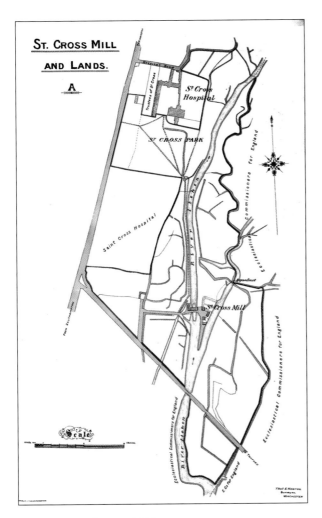

A PLAN OF ST CROSS IN 1904 SHOWS THE VARIOUS WATERCOURSES IN THE ST CROSS AREA. THE MEANDERING, ANCIENT COURSE OF THE ITCHEN IS FAR NARROWER THAN WYKEHAM'S DIVERSION TO POWER ST CROSS MILL. THE HOSPITAL BOUNDARY IS SHOWN IN RED.

Separated from the front room by a timber-framed spine wall are now two rear rooms: a bedroom and a kitchen. The kitchens are a modern introduction; Beaufort envisaged that his noble brethren would eat in the common hall. It is possible, though, that the rear rooms were always subdivided by light-weight partitions, as shown in the earliest surviving architectural survey of the hospital, drawn by the antiquary John Carter in 1789 (page 53). The larger rear room in each flat, with en-suite access to a privy, and a large window, was presumably the sleeping chamber; the smaller one was perhaps just a closet for storage. In the nineteenth century the smaller rooms were defined as 'sculleries', so the brothers may have brought food back to their rooms and washed their own dishes.

A GLIMPSE INTO THE ENTRANCE PASSAGE OF ONE OF THE GROUND-FLOOR APARTMENTS, WITH THE STAIR LEADING TO THOSE ON THE FIRST FLOOR.

in fours, each group having a common entrance off the quadrangle. Inside, there are doors to right and left into the ground-floor apartments, and a staircase leading to first-floor apartments of similar plan, though slightly larger because they oversail the stairwells.

The layout of each apartment was also standardised and has remained almost unchanged to this day. The main room is at the front, overlooking the quadrangle, and originally heated by a wide fireplace; the stone chimneys are a much admired external feature of the brothers' range. Beside the chimney is a wide window, originally with sociably disposed window-seats either side.

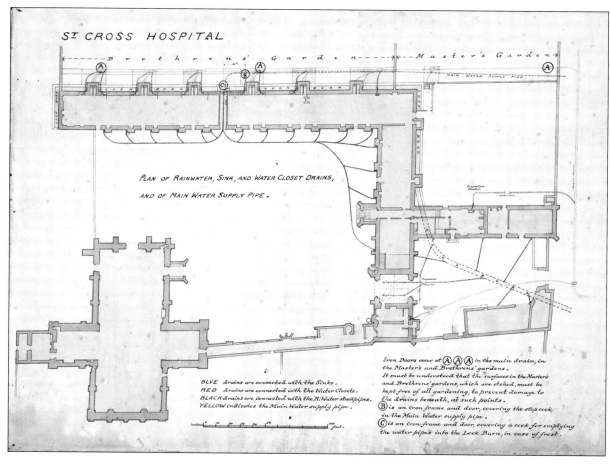

▲ A nineteenth-century plan of the hospital's drains shows in pale blue the course of the Lockburn, in use from 1450 until the late 1870s.

◄ A fifteenth-century fireplace, retained as an architectural feature (the rooms are now centrally heated).

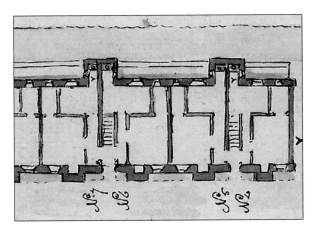

▲ Four ground-floor apartments in 1789 in a detail from John Carter's plan of the hospital (see page 93).

▶ The view from one of the ground-floor privies, little changed since the fifteenth century. Some of them even retain their original doors.

◀ Garderobe towers at the rear of the west range. The Lockburn flows along the back of the building, behind the grey coped wall.

Curiously, it is the privies that have survived with fewest changes. They still serve their original purpose. Beaufort would have called them 'garderobes': they were not 'water closets', as the concept of a flush toilet lay far in the future. But at the rear of the building, straddling the party walls between adjacent apartments, were projecting 'garderobe towers', built in stone and flint but with brick internal partitions, each tower containing four privies. They operated on the gravity principle, with simple wooden seats over the flowing Lockburn. Because the privies were on two levels, careful planning was required: those on the ground floor were smaller, with brick partition walls at the rear, behind which were the chutes from the first-floor privies. So the residents of the first-floor apartments enjoyed closets twice the size of those below, with windows in the outer wall rather than tucked into the sides. When mains drainage came to Winchester in the late 1870s the privies were plumbed into the city's sewerage system.

BEAUFORT REMODELS THE HALL

The hall existed around a century before Beaufort's works, having been erected by Master John of Edington mainly for his own use. Beaufort, not of course a master, had his own ideas and it was perhaps then that the emphasis changed, the hall now being intended to serve as the common dining hall for the Almshouse of Noble Poverty. The thirteen poor men of Henry of Blois's foundation were probably still required to eat in their own hall.

The most impressive changes were to the roof. Tree-ring dating has now conclusively proved that this was constructed in Beaufort's time, i.e. the 1440s. The earlier roof may have failed; certainly, rebuilding it also allowed the new roof to continue the exact height and pitch of the adjacent brothers' north range. The most eye-catching features of the present four-bay roof, which is built of oak throughout, are the great four-centred arched trusses that span the hall. These are in fact each formed from four arch-braces whose curves continue smoothly from one to the next. Their purpose was structural rather than decorative: they support the principal rafters which form the

▲ THE HALL ROOF IS SUPPORTED ON ANGEL CORBELS HOLDING, ALTERNATELY, THE ARMS OF CARDINAL BEAUFORT AND THOSE OF THE KING.

main articulation of the roof triangle, and into which two tiers of moulded purlins are tenoned. The purlins are in turn braced by arch-braces in the plane of the roof, the top tier being inverted, giving the impression of huge curved crosses. There is one additional refinement; the rafter feet are concealed behind a wooden frieze that runs along the wall-head. It is decorated with trefoiled panels.

Beaufort's involvement is clearly proclaimed by means of the angel corbels bearing his coat of arms, alternating with the royal arms. This is a typical fifteenth-century idea. There is some surviving original paint on the angels, particularly

▶ CARDINAL BEAUFORT'S NEW OAK ROOF DOMINATES THE BRETHREN'S HALL

in the crevices of their wing feathers, but the shields have been repainted. Beaufort's arms are, thanks to his royal parentage, almost the same as those of the king of England, differentiated by an edge of alternate blue-and-white stripes, known in heraldry as a 'bordure gobony'. The corner corbels are different, featuring angels blowing musical instruments. Those at the west end of the hall are half-covered by the floor of the gallery that was added after Beaufort's time. Not content with displaying his arms on the angel corbels, the cardinal also reglazed the hall windows with his arms, badge, and personal motto, *A honor et lyesse*. Only reinstated fragments now survive in the more protected tracery at the top of the windows; the glass in the main lights was probably smashed up during the Commonwealth. As a bishop and royal relative, Beaufort would have been doubly suspect.

▲ Heraldic glass in the tracery lights of the Brethren's Hall, with Beaufort's arms (surrounded by his cardinal's hat and tassels) and his motto *A honor et lyesse*.

▲ The corner corbels feature angels blowing musical instruments.

▲ THE HALL PORCH WAS ADDED BY CARDINAL BEAUFORT.

In the centre of the hall is a raised hearth, on which is now stacked a heap of logs like an unlit open fire. A charming painting of the brothers' Christmas celebrations in 1851, however, shows them warming themselves from the radiant heat of glowing charcoal heaped up on a large metal dish. Given the absence of any kind of louvre in Beaufort's roof, this was probably the type of heating that he provided for his new brethren. It is somewhat surprising that he did not introduce a conventional fireplace along one of the side walls.

Cardinal Beaufort also remodelled the west end of the hall's original tunnel vaulted basement, inserting a new cellar. Its original entrance, seldom used, is beneath the porch stairs with which it is clearly contemporary. Beaufort's cellar is very elegant indeed. Internally it is a perfect square, determined by the combined width of the two earlier tunnel vaults which it replaced. This explains why its length is unrelated to the bay structure of the earlier hall. Its most spectacular feature is its vault, springing from a single, central pillar. The ribs are four-centred in profile, matching the doors

◀ THE VAULT OF CARDINAL BEAUFORT'S HALL PORCH, WITH A DISPLAY OF HIS COAT OF ARMS AT THE CENTRE.

▶ BEAUFORT'S BEER CELLAR. THE DOOR ON THE LEFT LED UP TO THE BUTTERY WHERE DRINK WAS SERVED. THE ONE AT THE FAR END OPENS INTO THE REMAINS OF THE EARLIER, FOURTEENTH-CENTURY CELLARAGE.

and window openings of all Beaufort's work at the hospital. The fine stone floor is higher than its original level, concealing the bases of the central pillar and the wall responds.

As well as the door beneath the porch, two other doors lead out of the cellar. One leads to a stair to the kitchen wing, the other enters one of the earlier tunnel vaults. The cellar's most unusual feature is its fireplace, something rarely found in a cellar. Possibly a subsequent insertion, it was presumably intended as a means of climate control rather than for the comfort of the cellar master.

THE KITCHEN AND GUEST LODGINGS

As we have seen, the hall's original kitchen was probably a free-standing building reached from the external door at the north end of the cross-passage. Beaufort replaced it by a kitchen that was linked to the hall by an enclosed passage within the service wing running northwards from the corner of the hall. The kitchen impresses by its volume, being open to the very roof timbers of the north range which otherwise is two-storeyed. The roof is original but the windows were rebuilt in Bath stone

▲ THE KITCHEN, MUCH REBUILT IN THE NINETEENTH CENTURY.

by Butterfield in the nineteenth century, replacing a simpler design. Though the kitchen apparatus looks so medieval, in fact very little of the original hearth survives. Apart from the bread oven on the east side, everything else, including the chimney-hood, its beam, and the kitchen range below, results from a major refurbishment in 1860. But surviving from an earlier period is the lead pump, installed during the mastership of Henry Compton, *c.*1670; the sink is probably of the same date.

Next to the kitchen passage, between the kitchen and the hall, are two other smaller service rooms. They are now called the 'bread room' and the 'meat room' but their function seems to have changed: an account roll of 1451 calls them the 'buttery' and the 'pantry', and this is how they are still labelled in John Carter's plan of the hospital in 1789. Rather confusingly, the buttery is now called the 'bread room', and large ventilated cupboards show that it was indeed used for the storage of bread for a time. It leads directly from the hall, via a new door that Beaufort inserted next to the screens, and there is an additional door from the passage. In the corner of this room is a flight of steps down to Beaufort's cellar, proof that this was indeed the buttery (from French *bouteillerie*), the place where

◀ THE 'MEAT ROOM' (ORIGINALLY THE PANTRY), NOW USED FOR A DISPLAY OF MEDIEVAL AND POST-MEDIEVAL KITCHENWARE.

bottles were prepared for serving. The 'meat room' at the south end of the kitchen was originally the pantry (the 'bread room', French *paneterie*) but in the nineteenth century was used for hanging meat carcases on the hooks suspended from the ceiling; the cellar below acted as a chill store. The iron shutters of the meat room have now partly been replaced by glazed panels, allowing visitors to view a fine display of early kitchen equipment and other curiosities. These include leather beer jugs ('jacks') which, from their profile, appear to be Tudor. They form part of a group of objects which in the nineteenth century were displayed in the hall as the gift of Henry Beaufort: the beer jacks, a pair of candlesticks, and two old wooden salt cellars. The 'Beaufort Chair', now in the church, on which the master traditionally sits at the installation of a new brother, is seventeenth-century and could not possibly date from the cardinal's time.

The kitchen wing was soon extended northwards right up the west side of the entrance courtyard that is seen today. This range originally comprised accommodation on both floors in the form of a series of heated chambers. There was also a garderobe at the north end, served by a diversion of the Lockburn. Presumably the chambers, still in use as 'lodging rooms' in the late 1660s, were meant for well-to-do visitors to the hospital.

THE HUNDRED MENNE'S HALL

A hall in which the hundred poor men received their daily sustenance was certainly in existence by the late fourteenth century when Wykeham was carrying out his inquisition into the state of the hospital. As already noted, at that time the *Hundredemenhalle* was aligned to the master's hall. It probably occupied the site of the fifteenth-century range that runs westward from the present Brethren's Hall. This location was incompatible with Beaufort's plans, and he must have rebuilt the Hundred Menne's Hall where it is now. The style of a blocked doorway on the west side of the building supports this conjecture. The hall's south gable wall was rebuilt above ground level in the 1660s, but the way the original footings are integral with the adjacent boundary wall at the south-east corner proves the hall was never longer than it is today. The boundary wall was originally the side of a building (perhaps a service wing) standing south-east of the main hall, as shown by its plinth and the survival of an external doorway. From 1792 the Hundred Menne's Hall served as the hospital's brewhouse; at that date various other service buildings prolonged it to the south. They were demolished at the end of the nineteenth century.

BEAUFORT'S ACHIEVEMENT

The most obvious display of Beaufort's prestige is of course the tower that bears his name. As we have seen, the cardinal rebuilt the earlier gate-tower of John de Campeden. He firmly set his own stamp upon it, for as they enter the hospital precincts visitors immediately see not only a display of Beaufort's heraldry in the spandrels of the gate, but also a statue of the cardinal in the niche above.

▲ BEAUFORT'S COAT OF ARMS IN THE SPANDRELS OF THE MAIN GATE.

▲ STATUE OF CARDINAL BEAUFORT ON THE NORTH FACE OF HIS TOWER.

For a few brief years Cardinal Beaufort's new foundation rapidly expanded. There was a full complement of thirty-five brothers by 1451, and their names are known. Three of them were Wykehamists. Interestingly, the first brothers appear to have been appointed as early as 1445, before the buildings were even completed, presumably occupying apartments as they became available. By 1449 a second generation of brothers was emerging, when Richard Morris ('Morreys') replaced Henry Chambre. Perhaps the most interesting of these original Brothers of Noble Poverty is John Newles, who is commemorated by a brass now under the pews at the west end of the church. He died on 11 February 1453 and the inscription says that he was 'Born in Beaune, squyer and servant more than xxx yere unto Harry Beauford, Busshop and Cardinal'.

Some insight into the life of the hospital is provided by the account roll of 1451. This gives a detailed account of the new foundation's income from various manors and churches. It continues with a 'view of the state of the house of the new foundation' in that year. Although these are nothing more than itemised accounts similar to those previously kept by the St Cross steward, they do provide a glimpse of the hospital's affairs. The hospital was managed by Thomas Forest, and the officials of Beaufort's almshouse included two 'chaplains of the Lord Cardinal', three stewards, Robert Gooderegrome the butler, a cook and his

▲ JOHN BUCKLER'S WATERCOLOUR OF THE BEAUFORT TOWER, 1829.

servant, a barber, an auditor and five legal advisors. Also splendidly recorded is the provision of the gowns that since 1881 have again been worn by the Brothers of Noble Poverty. In 1450–51 over £14 was spent on dark red coloured cloth, purchased 'to make thirty-eight gowns this year'. Furthermore, William the Broderer was paid 30s 2d for embroidering on them the badge of the Cardinal's Hat (*les Cardinalhattes*) in silver thread and black and white silk. The work took four weeks, during which time William and his servant were lodged at the hospital's expense. The thirty-eight gowns cost a total of £21 17s 7d. This is a very large sum, a little more than the master's stipend and clothing allowance, and it is inconceivable that the operation was repeated every year. It was probably intended that new gowns would be provided when needed for new brethren or as replacements for those that wore out. So we may imagine the brothers parading in their brand new gowns, perhaps in time for the

anniversary of Cardinal Beaufort's death (his *obit*) on 11 April 1451. That was a magnificent event involving the ringing of bells and the lighting of a large number of wax candles, and a special payment 'to the chaplains, clerks, brethren and sisters as well of the New Foundation as of the Old Foundation': it was tactful not to alienate Henry of Blois's black brothers. The whole affair cost £3 15s 8d.

Well might the three sisters wear the same gowns as the brethren, and celebrate the cardinal's *obit* in style: they still had to wash the brothers' clothes. Perhaps they complained of the inadequacy of the facilities originally provided, for in 1451 Robert Sabale, mason, was employed in installing what the accounts call a *cacabus* in the sisters' house. The Latin word usually means 'cooking pot', but the context suggests a copper for laundry work, particularly as a plumber was employed in the associated leadwork and to install a sink 'for washing the brethren's clothes'.

▲ BISHOP WILLIAM WAYNFLETE SALVAGED WHAT HE COULD OF HIS PREDECESSOR'S ALMSHOUSE.

the Almshouse of Noble Poverty were also under threat, but the 1450 act specifically exempted St Cross and, not surprisingly, Eton College, which Henry had founded in 1440. Several other institutions were also exempt. Nevertheless, the hospital must have felt vulnerable; and there were legal concerns. The Almshouse of Noble Poverty had not been properly established as a corporate body. A few months after recovering from his two-year bout of insanity Henry VI determined to rectify matters. The text of a patent roll issued at Westminster on 8 April 1455 goes straight to the point. His great-uncle's intention was to found an almshouse of thirty-five men and three women within the old hospital precincts but its income was in the hands of the master alone, and the fact that two foundations were involved, and the income thus 'confused', was leading to strife amongst the brethren. There was every likelihood of the Beaufort foundation being 'brought to desolation'. In short, 'the almshouse had not been founded', so the king announced his intention of allowing Beaufort's successor as bishop of Winchester, William Waynflete, to create a 'New Almshouse of Noble Poverty', whose aims were almost as before, with the additional refinement that amongst the duties of the warden, three chaplains, thirty-five brothers, and three women was 'to pray for the good estate of the king and his soul after death, and for the soul of the cardinal'. The endowments that Beaufort had provided were currently bringing in an annual revenue of £158 13s 4d; the king now granted to the hospital the right to acquire properties that would yield a further £300 per annum. Five years later, in 1460, Bishop Waynflete drew up the charter of foundation in accordance with the royal wishes. For a few brief months the future of the Almshouse of Noble Poverty must have seemed assured.

Other aspects of the 1451 accounts show, alas, that the new foundation's affairs were not in such good heart. It has been calculated that the accounts show a total expenditure of £307 14s 5d, with a total income of £183 13s 4d, leaving a deficit of just over £124. The main problem was that the income was likely to be reduced still further, owing to the political uncertainties of the day. Henry VI needed money to carry on his French wars, and in 1450 he managed, by means of an Act of Resumption, to claw back some of the lands that he had previously disposed of. The manors that provided funding for

Chapter 6

THE END OF THE MIDDLE AGES 1485–1535

Cardinal Beaufort must have hoped that his Almshouse of Noble Poverty would endure to the end of time. Alas, the careful arrangements that he had made for its financial support proved short-lived. The crisis came in 1461 with the accession of the Yorkist king Edward IV. Many of the manors and lands that Beaufort had acquired to fund the almshouse had formerly belonged to the powerful Yorkist Montagu and Neville families. With Edward on the throne, Alice Montagu obtained licence to repossess the estates that had belonged to her grandfather. The foundation's income was drastically reduced. There was little that Bishop Waynflete, a Lancastrian supporter, could do.

REDUCTION IN SCALE

On Henry VII's accession in 1485, Waynflete made one last attempt at preserving Beaufort's foundation in vestigial form. In August 1486 he issued a charter. Through the machinations of successive people, the 'lordships, rents, tenements, and possessions' intended to provide financial support had been utterly taken away. Waynflete's only option was to reduce his predecessor's almshouse to the bare minimum. Henceforth there would be two brothers charged with saying prayers for the cardinal in perpetuity, like the old almsmen, but differently clad (no more dark red gowns). There would also be a chaplain. The brothers would receive an annual stipend of 73s 4d, the chaplain a little more (£4). Any surplus funds would be kept in reserve. The brothers would live in the

hospital and their quarters would be kept in good repair.

This was a sad end to Beaufort's high hopes. It was the end, too, of the short-lived experiment in gender equality, for we hear no more of the sisters. The accommodation that Beaufort had provided for thirty-eight people was clearly far in excess of requirements. We may assume that it was at this time that the thirteen men of Henry of Blois's hospital moved into the quadrangle, and the old buildings east of the church were demolished.

THE PARISH OF ST FAITH

Not surprisingly, people often refer to the hospital's 'chapel', but this is incorrect: it has always been known as the church (*ecclesia* in the *St Cross Register*). Furthermore, since 1446 the church has had a dual function: as the place where the brothers still worship daily, and also as the parish church of St Faith, named after a late third-century virgin martyr from southern France. Winchester's original church of St Faith was located between Sparkford (modern St Cross) and Winchester, at the fork in the road where two Roman roads divide, now St Cross Road and Kingsgate Road. The date of St Faith's Church is unknown, but the first recorded rector, John Bellegambe, died in 1287. Even though there has been no church building on the site for over five hundred years the burial ground remains in use. In the eighteenth century the hospital reserved the right to burials there. When Cardinal Beaufort established the Almshouse of Noble

◀ DESPITE THE HOSPITAL'S FINANCIAL DIFFICULTIES, NICHOLAS BEDFORD GAVE THIS WINDOW DEPICTING POPE GREGORY IN 1480.

▼ ANOTHER LATE FIFTEENTH-CENTURY WINDOW PORTRAYS THE VIRGIN MARY, PART OF A CRUCIFIXION GROUP.

Poverty he assigned to it the income from St Faith's Church, which thenceforth was incorporated with the hospital; the cardinal and his successor bishops of Winchester retained the right to appoint the incumbent. It seems possible that the church remained in use until the end of the fifteenth century, served by priests from the hospital. By the early sixteenth century St Faith's appears to have been in poor repair. There is some rather dubious historical evidence that the parish was formally joined to St Cross in 1507; its old church was probably demolished within a year or two. When the antiquary John Leland visited Winchester in 1538 he claimed that the 'fair church of St Faith' had been taken down in Fox's episcopate (1501–28). This seems probable, though there is no mention of the fact in the bishop's register.

Various items in St Cross Church are claimed to have been recycled from St Faith's, though this is pure supposition and some items might have come from elsewhere within St Cross Church. Flanking the chancel are two stone screens. Both show signs of having been adapted to suit their present location. The one on the south side is surmounted by an open arcade with tall pinnacles that have clearly been cut down to fit within the arch. The screen incorporates a low shelf-like credence table, the end adorned with a rather battered relief of an eagle with a scroll (the symbol of St John the Evangelist); a canopy above the shelf has regrettably been hacked back. The

north screen dates from the later fifteenth century and has statuary niches. It is altogether more elaborate than the south screen, a very beautiful, overlooked item of medieval craftsmanship. It appears to have been created to fit within an arch as now, but again the pinnacles are truncated, proving it is not in its original position. Like the south

▲ THE SOUTH CHANCEL SCREEN, RECYCLED EITHER FROM ST FAITH'S CHURCH OR FROM ANOTHER LOCATION AT ST CROSS.

▶ THE NORTH SCREEN. THE NICHES OF THE MIDDLE TIER WOULD HAVE HELD STATUES.

▲ THE WEST END OF THE CREDENCE TABLE, WITH THE EAGLE SYMBOL OF ST JOHN THE EVANGELIST.

▶ THE RE-USED LATE TWELFTH-CENTURY PURBECK MARBLE FONT, PERHAPS ALSO FROM ST FAITH'S CHURCH.

screen, it was perhaps recycled at the Reformation. The font is also said to have come from St Faith's. The bowl is made of Purbeck marble and, with its carved tendrils of curling 'Winchester acanthus' foliage, is twelfth-century; it sits on a post-medieval base.

ROBERT SHERBORNE

In 1492 one of St Cross's most distinguished masters was appointed, Robert Sherborne. Born in Basingstoke, he was educated at Winchester College, then, whilst still at New College, Oxford, obtained a prebend (canonry) at Salisbury Cathedral. Further honours came his way when, aged around thirty-two, he became Archbishop Morton's secretary. Soon he was made archdeacon of Taunton, then dean of St Paul's. Then in 1505, while still master of St Cross, he was elected bishop of St David's, but was translated to Chichester in 1508, where he remained until his death in 1545. Given this energetic life it is surprising that he had any time to devote to St Cross, yet he retained the mastership until 1508, and literally left his mark

on the hospital with signed building works. Most obvious are two fireplaces in his own lodgings, now the porter's lodge. Both bear his initials, his personal motto *Dilexi sapientiam* ('I have loved wisdom'), and the date *Anno Domini 1503*, written in the old form of the Arabic numerals that were then just beginning to replace cumbersome Roman ones. Sherborne probably merely upgraded the fireplaces using flues that were integral with Beaufort's reconstruction of the tower. There is a fireplace in the first-floor 'muniment room' over the gate passage and it is unlikely that in the mid-fifteenth century the master's lodgings would not have had proper heating. Sherborne's motto and the Arabic date 1497 also occur in window panes in the kitchen passage at St Cross. These panes were presumably salvaged from elsewhere (perhaps the master's lodgings), for the kitchen wing had been built forty years earlier.

▼ HENRY VIII AND BISHOP ROBERT SHERBORNE. A PAINTING BY LAMBERT BARNARD AT CHICHESTER CATHEDRAL. EVEN IN LATER LIFE SHERBORNE LIKED TO PLACE HIS INITIALS ON HIS WORKS: BY THEN HE HAD ADOPTED A NEW MOTTO, *OPERIBUS CREDITE* (BELIEVE IN HIS WORKS).

▲ Robert Sherborne's initials, motto, and the date A.D. 1503, carved on a fireplace in the porter's lodge.

▲ Robert Sherborne's initials, abbreviated motto, and the Arabic date 1497 in the kitchen passage.

The Ambulatory

The most ambitious of Sherborne's projects at St Cross was the 'ambulatory', a first-floor gallery between the church and the master's lodgings, with a walk-way beneath. Subsequent additions and alterations have turned it into something of an architectural hotch-potch. Originally it was elegantly simple. Its rear, east wall was already in place, being probably the boundary wall built by de Campeden in the late fourteenth century, or perhaps its later replacement. The front of the new gallery was supported on an open timber arcade whose main structural members were square posts, supported on a low stylobate wall. Between the posts was a series of shallow four-centred arches neatly decorated with cusped daggers and quatrefoils. The original framing of the upper storey, slightly jettied towards the quadrangle, survives only at the south end, everything else being replaced in a very flimsy construction.

The arcade was articulated by two octagonal stair turrets of brick and checker flint and a central brick oriel (a projecting bay window). The oriel was supported on twin brick arches and a central pier whose capital, replaced in 1939, bears Sherborne's motto and initials. He was determined that this building should be signed like all his other contributions to the hospital.

The symmetry of the ambulatory was compromised by later changes. In the sixteenth century the two timber arches between the north stair turret and the master's lodgings were replaced in brick. More extensive changes were undertaken by Master Henry Compton in 1675, probably necessary because of dilapidations during the Commonwealth. A contemporary account refers to 'The Rebuilding & Mending the falling Gallery over the Cloysters' during Compton's mastership. This suggests that he was responsible for the spindly framing of the upper storey; the original close studding survives only in the southernmost bay. Compton seems to have remodelled the central oriel, which bears his name. He probably also added the stone-built porch-like structure on the south side of the north stair turret, whose first floor presumably contained the 'chamber' mentioned in the account of Compton's works. This addition was capped by crenellation, which was also then added to the earlier brick wing on the other side of the stair turret to provide visual cohesion. The ambulatory has been further modified since Compton's day: in the nineteenth century the bay between the remains of the south turret and the

▲ The ambulatory. The stone structure near the north end was probably added by
Master Henry Compton c.1675, who also rebuilt the timber framing of most of the façade.

North end of the ambulatory showing two additions flanking the north stair turret: (left) the brick replacement of
two timber arches and (centre) the stone 'porch' and first-floor chamber, probably added by Master Henry Compton.

church was bricked up to form a boiler-room. In modern times the bottom of most of the posts was cut off and new feet were spliced on. In order to support the posts the stylobate wall had to be raised higher. All these changes have left a most intriguing building.

A number of unfounded suggestions have been made regarding the ambulatory, notably that the upper floor was an infirmary for sick brothers. This idea was first put about by the Winchester historian John Milner in 1799. The notion of a Nightingale style ward in the hospital is anachronistic and illogical, for the brethren enjoyed their own individual quarters, and in sickness would have remained in their own rooms, as if in a private hospital, not lined up in a long first-floor chamber. Nor was the north end of the gallery a 'nuns' room' as it was called in the later nineteenth century. Those 'nuns' (in reality the sisters of Beaufort's foundation) had long vanished from the scene.

The ambulatory is, in fact, a fairly typical example of an early Tudor 'long gallery', allowing the master and his household to walk in the dry and, probably, to get to the church sheltered from

▲ DETAIL OF THE SUPPORTING PILLAR TO THE ORIEL. THE CAPITAL WITH SHERBORNE'S MOTTO AND INITIALS WAS REPLACED IN 1939; THE OWL ABOVE IT WAS INTRODUCED IN 1969.

the weather. Access to the church was certainly possible at ground level, through a small fourteenth-century doorway that was perhaps inserted into the transept's north gable wall when a walk-way from the master's lodgings was first created. On the upper storey the gallery led to one of the Romanesque windows in the north wall of the transept. Although it is just possible that the master used this as a pew, allowing him to attend services without leaving his home, he could not have seen anything from there; it is much more likely that there was a wooden stair in the transept so he could go to services in the choir without venturing outside. But the main purpose of the gallery was as an internal promenade for its own sake. When he became bishop of Chichester, Sherborne added a similar gallery to his palace there.

One modification to the Brethren's Hall might have taken place in Sherborne's time, namely the creation of the western gallery. As originally built, the cross-passage was separated from the hall by wing walls and a free-standing central section, with doorways later inserted into the gaps. Even after Beaufort reroofed the hall, the passage remained open to the roof. In the late medieval period, a

◀ THE ORIEL WINDOW IN THE AMBULATORY, ORIGINALLY CENTRALLY PLACED WITH FIVE BAYS OF TIMBER ARCADING EITHER SIDE.

substantial beam was placed along the top of the screens, another was set on corbels in the hall's west wall, and joists were laid between them forming a simple rectangular gallery, accessed via an inserted door from the first floor of Beaufort's kitchen wing. The function of the gallery is uncertain, but it is not impossible that musicians played or sang from it from time to time, as is popularly believed.

BISHOP FOX

The hospital's interests had always been well served by the bishops of Winchester, who exercised the functions of overseers and were responsible for appointing the master. Bishop Richard Fox showed a particular interest in the hospital (even perhaps acting as master during a long interregnum between Robert Sherborne and John Claymond) and his influence is visible today. Like his predecessors, Fox had played an active role in the affairs of the realm. He was chief advisor to Henry VII, negotiated the marriage treaty of Katharine of Aragon and Prince Arthur, and after the prince's death played a role in the long betrothal of Katharine and the future Henry VIII. He was bishop successively of Exeter, Bath and Wells, then Durham, before being translated to Winchester in 1501. Soon after his

arrival he began to remodel the presbytery of his cathedral, and its aisles. Meanwhile he founded Corpus Christi College, Oxford; John Claymond became its first president, whilst continuing as master of St Cross. By 1516 Fox was more or less permanently resident in Winchester. It was in this final period of his life that he used some of the huge income that he derived from his episcopal estates for the embellishment of the hospital.

Fox's greatest gift was the refurbishment of the east end of the church, for which he commissioned a small, enclosed choir. It occupied the west bay of the east arm, and comprised wonderful wooden stalls in the latest Renaissance style of which the bishop was so fond. We know the general configuration of the stalls from John Carter's plan of 1789, and they appear as distant details in a number of antiquarian drawings. Sadly the stalls were butchered in the nineteenth century, several of their individual components being dispersed in different parts of the church.

The most substantial surviving elements are found in the chancel. Either side are the cut-down remains of the rear seating, beneath coved canopies. Above them, rather incongruously spanning between the piers, are the remains of openwork friezes. They are in two tiers separated by a moulded, horizontal rail, which was originally attached to the front of the coving, so that the lower tier hung down in front of the canopy, the pendant posts defining the individual seats. Just six seats have survived on either side, part of a longer run of seating that curved inwards as return stalls at the west end. The desks in front of the surviving seats, with their linen-fold panels, also came from the Renaissance stalls, but they have lost their most engaging features, the dolphins that adorned their bench-ends. Fortunately two dolphins survive intact on the desks flanking the entrance to the south-east chapel. These desks were formed from a single one that was sawn in half and turned end to end so the bench-ends face each other across the aisle. The chapel's entrance screen and door are in the same style as the stalls and must also be Bishop Fox's work (the cresting is surely an addition). The screen cannot have been recycled from the stalls as it was designed for the space it now occupies.

▲ BISHOP FOX. A NINETEENTH-CENTURY LITHOGRAPH OF A CONTEMPORARY PORTRAIT.

SURVIVING ELEMENTS OF THE RENAISSANCE STALLS ON THE SOUTH SIDE OF THE CHOIR.

DOLPHIN BENCH-ENDS FLANKING THE ENTRANCE TO THE SOUTH-EAST CHAPEL.

▶ BISHOP FOX'S FAVOURITE PELICANS, A SYMBOL OF CHRIST'S SACRIFICE, ADORN HIS CHANTRY CHAPEL IN WINCHESTER CATHEDRAL.

It is of course the exquisite *cinquecento* detail that is the great joy of these stalls. The upper part of the stall canopies consisted of pinnacles marking the seat divisions, and, between them, openwork panels enclosing roundels. One of these features the image of the 'pelican in its piety': the bird pecking its breast and nourishing its young with drops of blood. This is an ancient Christian symbol for the sacrifice of Christ, which arose from a misinterpretation of the way pelicans groom themselves. It was a symbol dear to Bishop Fox's heart; he adopted it as his personal badge, and pelicans are to be found in great number adorning his chantry chapel in Winchester Cathedral. Equally attractive are the portrait busts at the ends of the pendant posts between each seat. They depict in the main prophets and sybils, the latter being female figures. Needless to say all kinds of folklore was subsequently attached to the images, and one of the figures used to be pointed out to visitors as a portrait of Anne Boleyn. This wonderful *all'antica* work is generally datable by its style to around 1520, and was the work of Franco-Italian carvers.

▲ THE REMAINS OF THE STALL CANOPIES ARE NOW FIXED TO THE WALLS
ABOVE THEIR ORIGINAL POSITIONS.

▲ CONJECTURAL RECONSTRUCTION BY PETER FERGUSON OF THE RENAISSANCE CHOIR STALLS FROM THE SOUTH-EAST.
© HUGH HARRISON CONSERVATION.

▶ Bishop Fox's stair in the corner of the Brethren's Hall.

▲ The figure of a prophet from the Renaissance stalls.

Bishop Fox's influence is visible in one other place. As already noted, access from the Brethren's Hall to the original master's lodgings consisted of a flight of stairs ascending to a high-level doorway into the south-west stair turret of the Beaufort Tower. Bishop Fox may actually occasionally have lived in the master's lodgings after Sherborne's departure, and perhaps found this circuitous arrangement irksome. It was almost certainly at his instigation that a new door was cut through the end wall of the hall, at the head of a new flight of steps. Being higher than their predecessor, these steps could no longer lie against the end wall. They would have intruded too much into the dais, so they were aligned to the side wall, partly blocking the end window and rendering its window-seat unusable. Fox's involvement in this project is indicated by his pelican symbol, now very worn, on the post at the bottom of the lattice-work handrail.

In 1524 John Incent became master. Once again, St Cross proved a useful rung in an prestigious ecclesiastical career, for he rose to be dean of St Paul's Cathedral between 1540–45, and in 1541 he founded Berkhamsted School in his native town. His Latin motto, which became that of the school, *virtus laudata crescit* ('greatness that is praised increases'), is to be found in the brothers' billiards room, on the frieze of recycled panelling that Incent had perhaps originally installed in the earlier master's lodgings east of the Beaufort Tower. Incent endowed the school with properties in Sparkford, though after his departure disputes arose as to exactly which tenements were involved.

A snapshot of life in the hospital at this time is provided by the account roll of his steward, William Pare, for 1526–7. The income from the various manors and churches is carefully presented, together with gains from the sale of surplus produce, such as sheepskins, wood, suet, and the possessions of a deceased brother. The income came to nearly £500, a profit of about £90 over expenses. The record of salaries show that the church was well staffed: fifteen chaplains, and clerks sang the services, together with boy choristers under the care of a schoolmaster who received an additional 10s 9d a year. The maintenance of the choristers cost £5 17s 6½d. Amongst the outgoings were regular payments to just eleven brethren, including a clothing allowance. There were four or five ordinary servants, a common barber and laundress, and a washer of vestments. The hundred poor received £6 18s 8d in alms. The expenditure on food is interesting: white and red herrings, sticklebacks, mushrooms. 'Divers kinds of wine' were bought at Southampton, as well as figs; spices were brought from London. There was also the cost of 'coal' (charcoal) and firewood, and an inexplicable payment for 'food bought for the gulls'. The resident moles were less fortunate, and the mole-catcher received a shilling for exterminating them. A dovecote is mentioned. The remains of a circular dovecote may still be seen in the north-east corner of the Master's Garden; whether this is the one in existence in the sixteenth century is uncertain. Interestingly, the dovecote mentioned in the accounts was let out to rent, though a reduction was granted because the pigeons were 'expended within the house'.

THE REFORMATION

In 1534 Thomas Cromwell had been appointed Henry VIII's vicar-general, with authority to undertake a general visitation of any religious house. Although the Hospital of St Cross was not a monastery, it was nevertheless a religious establishment with a substantial income, and Master John Incent, his substantial body of chaplains and clerks (still praying for the soul of a Roman Catholic cardinal), and his brethren, had reason to be apprehensive. On 20 September 1535 Cromwell dispatched the unpleasant Dr Legh to Winchester to make a few routine enquiries: a training exercise, perhaps, for the closure of monasteries that began the following year. Incent

▲ BISHOP FOX'S PELICAN SYMBOL ADORNS THE BOTTOM POST OF THE STAIRCASE IN THE BRETHREN'S HALL.

seems to have been able to persuade Legh that the hospital was simply a benefice without the care of souls, and certainly not in any sense monastic. So the royal visitor took a careful look around and compiled a report, with recommendations. After a lengthy preamble that was probably standard text for all such documents, Legh got down to the real meat: all those who aspired to become brothers must be genuinely infirm, and the thirteen brethren of Henry of Blois's foundation should be fed and clothed rather than being offered cash in lieu of charity.

The question of the hundred poor men was more delicate. Legh concluded that they should not simply be fed at the outer gate as had evidently become the custom, but should sit down at table as the founder had specified. Care should be taken not to make them dependent on these charitable benefactions, and 'sturdy beggars' of the sort that often hung around such places should be driven away by force. He then stipulated that a suitable priest within the hospital should teach the brethren the Lord's Prayer and the Apostles' Creed in English, which all were to recite together daily in the church after their mid-day meal. Legh passed on the usual injunction that relics should not be displayed in the church; rather, any offerings that might have been made to saints should be given to the poor. Finally, the hospital was to have a library including the Old and New Testaments and the writings of the early Church Fathers.

Legh also stipulated that the foundation at St Cross should not be reduced in size. The choral foundation in particular appears to have been maintained. We know this because in the 1570s the names of some of the chaplains and clerks of the church were carved on the prayer desk now on the north side of the choir. At the head of the list, beneath the hospital's coat of arms, is 'Master Jhon [sic] Watson, Master of this Place'. All the first inscriptions were professionally done by the same carver; later graffiti on the desk are more amateurish. Then follows 'Sir Jhon Watson, Chanter'; 'Sir Henrie Watson, Steward'; 'Sir Ihon Wrighte, Curat'; 'Sir William Ley'; 'Richard Shere'; 'Walter Cheyny'; 'Henrye Kingewoode'; 'R. Ganiet, Singing-man, the year of Christ 1573'; and 'Morgaine Lydford 1575'.

▲ THE NAMES OF THE FOUNDATION IN 1572 AND LATER, CARVED ON ONE OF THE PRAYER DESKS.

The three Watsons were presumably all members of the same family. Master John Watson had become a canon of Winchester Cathedral in 1551 and was made master of St Cross eight years later. He spent much of his mastership sorting out financial irregularities perpetrated by his predecessor. In 1580 he was consecrated bishop of Winchester, but remained master for three more years, and at his death in 1584 he left a specific bequest to the St Cross brethren. His name lives on in a curious way; it is alleged that Sir Arthur Conan Doyle, visiting Winchester, took the name 'Dr Watson' from the bishop. The tradition was good enough for members of the Sherlock Holmes Society, who made a pilgrimage to St Cross in 1991 to see what they imagined was his autograph signature on the prayer desk.

The Hospital of St Cross was perhaps lucky to escape Legh's visitation unscathed. He closed down the hospital of Burton Lazars in Leicestershire, another twelfth-century foundation, in 1536 and appointed himself master the following year. By 1544 that hospital had been closed down. Even so, the Reformation must have affected St Cross Church more than the hospital's domestic buildings. The religious statuary that adorned the niches of the north chancel screen was probably torn down at the start of Edward VI's reign if not earlier, and the outline of the statues may still be seen in the medieval paintwork. The rood-loft was another casualty, and the sockets of the rood beam are still visible. The door from the aisle roof-space to the loft, whose outline is still visible in the church, must have been blocked at this time. A modern 'rood' spans the west arch of the tower, no longer featuring the Crucifixion group but the hospital's Jerusalem Cross. The older brothers must have been aghast at the transformation of their well-loved Catholic church.

Chapter 7

THE SEVENTEENTH AND EIGHTEENTH CENTURIES

It is ironic that we know most about the hospital in times of trouble, owing to the paperwork generated by enquiries such as Bishop Wykeham's inquisition into the malfeasance of earlier fourteenth-century masters. During the reign of Elizabeth and the early Stuarts the hospital's affairs seem to have progressed more smoothly. In those times successive masters were appointed as much by the monarch as by the bishop, and there was a slight hiccup at the start of James I's reign when George Brooke, who claimed to have been promised the mastership by the late queen, was tried for his involvement in the Bye Plot (an attempt to depose the king on religious grounds). On 5 December 1603 he was put to death on Winchester Castle Green on a scaffold that was allegedly placed so he could could be taunted by a distant view of the hospital and the fading dream of better things.

James I was also responsible for the appointment to the mastership of his former tutor, Sir Peter Young, in 1616. Young was of course a layman, and in any case this was a titular appointment: he was an old man of seventy-two and spent most of his time in Scotland or at the court. He entrusted the administration of the hospital to his son, John Young, the dean of Winchester. One of the more interesting documents in the cathedral library is the diary kept by Dean Young during his time in Winchester, in which he painstakingly records the income that he received from the hospital on his father's behalf, money that he dutifully forwarded

to Scotland. In 1621, for example, he sent £60 in gold to Sir Peter at Holyrood House.

Dean Young in turn left most of the running of the hospital to a certain 'Mr Wright', his chaplain and steward. Some improprieties may have taken place, for at Wright's death his widow burnt various papers, including the church's register of births, marriages, and deaths. A later chaplain wrote at the start of the replacement register, 'This Mr Wright dying, his widdow, whether out of fear of being brought to accounts, or out of obedience to his commands is uncertain, burnt all his papers, and amongst them the Register also.'

Sir Peter was succeeded by Dr Lewis, who has been described as 'a very cross and disagreeable person'. One of his first tasks was to reply to the visitation injunctions of Archbishop Laud, in 1632. The hospital's affairs were investigated in some detail. Of particular interest is the list of personnel: 'Our Hospital doth consist of a Master and 13 Brethren; a Chaplain and Steward; 12 Out-Brethren and 28 Out-Sisters that are not lodged in the House; and 2 Probationers.' No specific mention is made of the Hundred Men, who had been replaced by the 'out-brethren': men and women who lived in their own homes but were allotted a stipend by the hospital. As for Beaufort's foundation, it was defunct.

Dr Lewis's comments on the state of repair of the hospital and its church are illuminating. He had found the buildings in great ruin and dilapidation, but they were now 'in far better repair than they have been within the memory of man'. The roofs of the church's east arm and the nave aisle had been releaded, several windows previously blocked with boards and mortar had been opened up and glazed, an organ had been installed. The church had been 'repaved' presumably by relaying the medieval tiles. The floor of Beaufort's cellar had also been repaved, and all four sides of the quadrangle retiled. The brewhouse, which was located near the riverbank, had been repaired and retiled; so had the bakehouse in the outer court.

Dr Lewis added that no allowance for repairing the hospital buildings had been made by his predecessor, and that he had personally expended about £1,000 on repairs. The criticism of Dean Young is clear, and given that Lewis was a member of Dean Young's cathedral chapter, and that Young was also one of the archbishop's commissioners, his answers must have strained relations between the dean and his canon.

▲ Dr Lewis lived mainly at No. 9, The Close, where his house was rebuilt after the Restoration of the Monarchy in 1660.

There were greater storms on the horizon. When the monarchy gave way to the Commonwealth Lewis fled the country; his royalist views were too well known. He was replaced by the Member of Parliament for Winchester, John Lisle, who occupied the post for a few years before handing over control to the Parliamentarian lawyer John Cook. The latter's dubious claim to fame is that, as Parliament's Solicitor-General, he drew up the indictment that led to the execution of Charles I. As a proven regicide Cook came to a bad end, himself falling to the axe at Tyburn at the Restoration of Charles II. Pepys later saw his head in Westminster Hall. Dr Lewis, one of the few cathedral canons to have survived the Commonwealth (his old house was even rebuilt for him), was reinstated as master of St Cross, where he died in office in July 1667. He was buried in the centre of the choir.

Little is known of how the hospital fared during the Commonwealth. We must assume that the organ purchased by Dr Lewis perished. The puritans loathed organs, and in 1642 the cathedral organ was smashed up by Cromwellian soldiers, who rampaged through the streets tooting the pipes like trumpets. In 1644 church organs were specifically banned by a parliamentary ordinance. Two rather charming graves in the south-east chapel have survived from the Commonwealth, marking the burials of Susanna Laurence (aged three) and her younger brother George (aged eleven months). Their grieving parents ingeniously turned each of their names into a suitable Latin phrase: thus 'Susana Laurence' became *uas carne valens*, loosely translated as 'A flesh prevailing vessel found, beautified to lye under ground'; 'Georgius Laurentius' was re-ordered as *ego uti laurus rigens*, 'I under ly as laurel dry'.

Henry Compton

After forty years as master (if one includes his long exile) Dr Lewis was replaced by Henry Compton, youngest son of the second earl of Northampton. As a ten-year-old boy Henry had been present in the Royalist camp at Edgehill (October 1642), but his father was killed five months later at the battle of Hopton Heath. At the Restoration of the monarchy Henry followed a military career for a time, until Dean Fell of Christ Church, Oxford, persuaded him to take holy orders. His career was meteoric. Ordained in 1666, within months he was put forward as master of St Cross by the king, and instituted on 18 November 1667. How much time Compton spent in Winchester is uncertain. He appears to have lived mostly at Christ Church, where he was a canon and later sub-dean; in 1674 he was appointed bishop of Oxford. Nevertheless, his initials are to be found in four places around

◀ THE OUTER GATE, ORIGINALLY BY BEAUFORT, WAS REMODELLED BY HENRY COMPTON, WHO ADDED THE EXTENSION ON THE RIGHT, AT THE NORTH END OF THE HUNDRED MENNE'S HALL.

the hospital, suggesting more than mere repair. The letters 'HC' appear twice on an irregularly-shaped store-room next to the outer gate, at the north end of the Hundred Menne's Hall. One inscription also has the date 1675. The room fills the angle between the fifteenth-century gate and the hall, and intrudes slightly into the hall itself, and Compton inserted a lightweight partition shortening the north end of the hall by around six feet. The addition encroached slightly into the meadow north of the hospital precincts. Its purpose is uncertain, but the addition might conceivably have been intended as the first porter's lodge at a time when the room within the Beaufort Tower formed part of the master's lodgings.

A contemporary account says that Henry Compton 'rebuilt' the Hundred Menne's Hall. This cannot be strictly true, given the survival of a fifteenth-century doorway and windows in the west wall. In fact he merely rebuilt the hall's south gable wall on its original footings, marking his work by an inscribed stone in the south gable wall. Nevertheless, with modifications both at the north and the south end of the hall, Compton's works might well have been regarded as a reconstruction.

As already noted, Compton also rebuilt the upper floor of Sherborne's ambulatory, by then in a state of collapse. A contemporary account drawn up in 1676 by his steward, Alexander Marshall, mentions the sum of £50 for 'The Rebuilding & mending the falling Gallery over the cloysters, with new tymber & plastering & rafters & new lathing & tyleing all over from one end to the other & placeing & mending the wainscott, & a new chamber made in it.' This 'new chamber' probably formed part of the stone extension adjacent to the north stair turret. Compton's works on the ambulatory can be accurately dated by a stone below the central oriel window. It reads 'Henry Compton *Episcopus*', and although the year is not given it must have been 1675, the year when he was concurrently bishop of Oxford and master of St Cross. When in December of that year he was promoted to the see of London, he resigned the mastership.

◀ *HENRY COMPTON EPISCOPUS* (BISHOP) ON A STONE FORMING PART OF THE ORIEL WINDOW OF THE AMBULATORY.

Compton was a passionate gardener, though it is unlikely that he had the time or opportunity to indulge in such pursuits at St Cross. In later life he laid out the gardens of his palace at Fulham with an impressive variety of exotic plants and trees, many sent to him by correspondents in America, whose English colonies formed part of his diocese. It was at the time the most diverse botanical garden in England. As part of St Cross's 850th anniversary celebrations in 1986 the 'Compton Garden' was laid out in his memory, a delightful enclave in the north-east corner of the hospital precincts. Its carefully researched plantings include species that would have been introduced from North America to this country in Compton's own day. The garden was opened by Her Majesty Queen Elizabeth, the Queen Mother, on 8 July 1986.

During Compton's tenure the hospital was described by the cartographer Richard Blome in his *Britannia* (1673), including an early account of the famous Wayfarer's Dole: 'Near unto Winchester is St. Crosses Hospital, pleasantly seated on a fine River, and endowed with liberal maintenance for the relief of twelve poor men, called Brothers, having a Master, Steward, and Sub-officers; and here, according to the institution of the House, bread and drink is given to all Travellers that will require the same.'

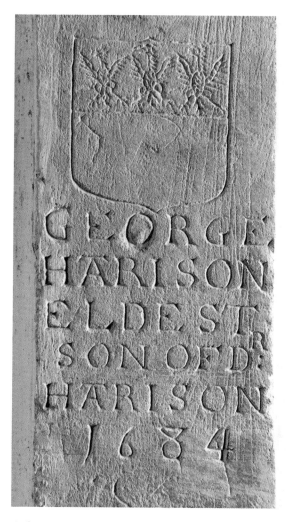

▲ Graffito in the hall, done by George Harison, the master's son.

◀ The view towards St Catherine's Hill from the 'Compton Garden', created in 1986 and named after Master Henry Compton, a passionate gardener.

ABRAHAM MARKLAND'S MASTER'S LODGE AND GARDEN

For the next eighteen years life the hospital's routine flowed on without incident under the relaxed administration of another Winchester Cathedral canon, Dr William Harison. The seeds of disaster were sown by the next master, Abraham Markland, appointed in 1694. Things got off to a bad start, when Harison's widow claimed tithes and other revenues due to her husband at the time of his death; she eventually won her case. Markland was an Oxford graduate with an interest in poetry, and in 1667, whilst at St John's College, had composed a work with the unwieldy title *Poems on his Majesties Birth and Restoration; His Highness Prince Rupert's and His Grace the Duke of Albemarle's Naval Victories; the Late Great Pestilence and Fire of London.* He married Catharine Pitt of Stratfield Saye, who died in 1693 at the age of fifty-six. Markland himself probably composed the epitaph on her ledger slab in the choir, which explains that

she died, presumably of a stroke, whilst hastening to church: 'snatched away not so much by apoplexy as exstasy' (*non tam apoplexia quam ecstasi correpta*).

Abraham Markland, who then married again, was evidently used to greater comfort than the late medieval master's lodgings could provide, and adapted several of the redundant brothers' quarters in the north-west corner of the quadrangle to gain more spacious accommodation. The apartments at the north end of the west side have been reinstated, but the north wing remains substantially as remodelled for Markland. The most striking room is the first-floor Trustees' Room, which has a good fireplace and a fine array of heraldic glass. On the ground floor, the panelling of the brothers' billiards room was perhaps recycled from the old master's lodgings east of the Beaufort Tower. As already noted, it was probably originally made in the second quarter of the sixteenth century for Master John Incent, whose motto it bears. Markland, another keen horticulturalist, would have appreciated the second motto, *dignus a dignis seminibus flos*, 'a worthy flower from worthy seeds'.

DAILY LIFE IN THE HOSPITAL

More controversial were Markland's attempts to sort out the duties and privileges of the hospital community. Although a constitution had been drawn up by Waynflete for the Almshouse of Noble Poverty, it was now represented by just two brothers and a chaplain: and for Henry of Blois's foundation there was merely the weight of convention. Markland was determined that things should be codified, so in the first year of his rule (1694–5), drawing on the expertise of old Mr Complin, who had been hospital steward for the past thirty-six years, he composed a document called the *Consuetudinarium* (in English, the 'Custumary'), which attempted to describe how things had traditionally been done at the hospital.

Some sections are uncontroversial and provide a fascinating snapshot of life at St Cross at the end

◀ THE ARMS OF BISHOP WILLIAM OF WYKEHAM, ENCIRCLED BY THE GARTER, IN THE TRUSTEES' ROOM.

of the seventeenth century. The hospital personnel was unchanged since Dr Lewis had described it to Thomas Legh 150 years previously, and Markland confirms that the old 'Hundred Hall' arrangement had given way to what he called an additional charity of twenty-eight out-sisters and twelve out-brethren. Their feeding arrangements are described in the past tense, suggesting that they no longer came to the hospital to receive their cuts of mutton, soup, bread, beer, pottage, and other delicacies. There is much detail about the brothers' food and drink, and this is emphatically in the present tense: they were allowed 'a pint of beer and a piece of bread at eight o'clock in the morning, a quart of beer and a piece of bread at dinner, a pint of beer and a piece of bread at three o'clock in the afternoon, and a quart of beer and a piece of bread at supper', though they were permitted to draw the entire ration in one go in the morning if they preferred. As for food, 'They have also forty-six and a half pounds of beef and forty-six and a half pounds of mutton allowed to them by the week, part whereof is boiled to make broth, the other part thereof, that is upon Sunday nights, is roaste.'

That was just the ordinary fare. Things got more lively on church feast days: at All Saints, Christmas, New Year's Day, Twelfth Night, and Candlemas they enjoyed 'extraordinary commons', and the night before they were allowed 'a fire of charcoal in the Common Hall, and one jack of six quarts and one pint of beer extraordinary, to drink together by the fire'. Then, on the feast-days themselves,

> . . . they have a fire at dinner and another at supper in the said hall : and they have a sirloin of beef roasted, weighing 46½lb., and three large mince pies, and plum broth, and three joints of mutton for their supper, and six quarts and one pint of beer extraordinary at dinner, and six quarts and one pint of beer after dinner, by the fireside ; six quarts and a pint at supper, and the like after supper.

There was provision for pancakes on Shrove Tuesday, roast chicken, further incredible quantities of beer, fish during Lent, and yet more beer . . . An allowance was given to each brother to pay the laundress, and the master was responsible for paying the barber 'for the trimming of the brothers'. Every time the hospital granted a new lease of one of its properties, the brothers were given a bonus of 2d in the pound out of the premium or 'fine' paid. 'And at Christmas, yearly, every brother hath a new gown made of black cloth . . .'

The Custumary included one important clause that was to spell disaster. 'It hath been the custom and usage, and is now, that the master should rule

◀ Life in the Brethren's Hall in the nineteenth century.

all persons in and belonging to the said Hospital and receive either by himself or his Steward all the profits and revenues thereof, with which he is to bear the whole charge of the house . . . and to keep the Church and House in sufficient repair, and the surplus, if any there be, he is to retain to himself.'

'He is to retain to himself.' There was the rub. It meant that successive masters could grow rich on the hospital revenues, provided they could convince themselves that they were feeding and clothing the brothers adequately. During the great chancery case of 1853 the Master of the Rolls commented that 'a more bare-faced and shameless document, in my opinion, than this *Consuetudinarium* could not have been framed ; nor could a more manifest, and probably wilful, breach of trust have been committed by the master and brethren.' Markland's Custumary was to dog the hospital for the next 150 years.

It would be unfair to brand Markland as merely intent on feathering his own nest. The Custumary included an increase in the allowance paid to the

▲ The Beaufort Tower and porter's lodge from the Compton Garden.

brethren, and during Markland's mastership the chaplain also received a pay rise. Markland acquired a reputation as a preacher, and the sermons that he delivered in Winchester Cathedral were published posthumously. Nor were Markland's horticultural skills forgotten, for at his death in 1728 a long epitaph on his ledger slab in the choir mentioned that 'he adorned this place with the amenity and elegance of gardens'. The implication would appear to be that he was the first to lay out the Master's Garden.

History got a gruesome revenge. On 2 June 1864 the Winchester antiquary Francis Baigent witnessed the opening of Abraham Markland's tomb, during alterations to the floor level of the chancel. He noted, 'there were the remains of the shroud folds visible, presenting a woollen appearance but turned perfectly black. The skull had fallen forward so that nothing could be seen of the jaw or teeth.' Nor did the first Mrs Markland escape Baigent's probings: 'a brick was removed from the top of a vault, directly under the place where Mrs Catharine Markland's slab existed. It was a single vault and contained the skeleton of a female. The teeth all remained in the lower jaw and seemed to be of a person about 40.' Baigent was generous in his assessment of the lady's age.

Two verbal sketches of the hospital have come down to us from Abraham Markland's mastership. In 1714 John Macky published his *Journey through England*. He described the Wayfarer's Dole, lamented the fact that the foundation was reduced to fourteen men, who 'wear black gowns, and go to prayers twice a day'. He commented that 'This Institution . . . hath fallen off from the first design; for there are seldom any gentlemen among them. The Brothers are put in at the pleasure of the Master, who lives like an Abbot; hath a very good apartment, with fine gardens, adorned with a canal and evergreens; with his coach-house and stables; and his income is computed to be a good £600 a year.'

A number of features in the Brethren's Hall perhaps date from the seventeenth century. The gallery at the west end of the hall was extended slightly into the body of the hall, and a projecting pulpit-like structure was formed by replacing the central joists with longer ones, cantilevered over the top of the screen; the constructional detail was

◀ THE COVED EXTENSION OF THE
GALLERY WAS PROBABLY ADDED IN
THE SEVENTEENTH CENTURY.

▲ AN EARLY, PERHAPS SEVENTEENTH-CENTURY WINDSOR CHAIR
IN THE BRETHREN'S HALL.

then concealed behind elegant coving. Perhaps it was then that the leather fire buckets were first suspended from the screen.

The hall also gained some furniture, notably three early chairs. One of them is amongst the earliest comb-back Windsor chairs in existence. The chairs appear in almost all the historic drawings and prints of the hall, evidence of an extraordinary continuity. The early Windsor chair was created for the senior brother, as is shown by the words carved on the underside of the seat, *In usum senioris fratris*.

THE EIGHTEENTH CENTURY

In 1724 Daniel Defoe's readers must have been entertained by his assessment of St Cross Hospital in his *Tour thro' the Whole Island of Great Britain*. He did not pull his punches, and after a description of the Wayfarer's Dole continued:

How the revenues of this hospital, which should maintain the master and thirty private gentlemen (whom they call Fellows, but ought to call Brothers), is now reduced to maintain only fourteen, while the master lives in a figure equal to the best gentleman in the country, would be well worth the inquiry of a proper visitor, if such can be named. It is a thing worthy of complaint when public charities, designed for the relief of the poor, are embezzled and depredated by the rich, and turned to the support of luxury and pride.

During the rest of the eighteenth century life flowed quietly on within the hospital precincts. The buildings deteriorated more and more and the church was evidently cold, inhospitable, and above all, moist. Markland's successor, the notorious pluralist John Lynch petitioned Bishop Hoadly, stating that, 'The Chapel of the Said Hospital is a very wet and damp place and the Brethren thereof are now and usually have been very ancient men and therefore cannot attend upon the service of Almighty God at Evening Prayer without manifest hazard and danger of their health and Lives.' The bishop agreed to a modification of the Custumary, and the daily services were reduced from two to a single attendance at eleven o'clock. Some minor building works appear to have occurred during Lynch's tenure, and a sheet of roofing lead now in the Brethren's Hall is his principal memorial at the hospital.

Lynch spent little or no time in Winchester, preferring to live at Lambeth, then, after the death of the archbishop his father-in-law, at Canterbury where Lynch had been dean since 1734. He died there in 1760, three years after an incapacitating stroke. He is remembered above all for his huge

▲ A FRAGMENT OF ROOFING LEAD COMMEMORATING THE ABSENTEE MASTER, JOHN LYNCH.

portfolio of benefices in an age where pluralism was not uncommon, and was lampooned in the anonymous *Life of Dean L—ch* (1748), in which it was alleged that ambition had driven him to marrying a wife who was 'exceedingly plain in Person and much deformed', and that he rated his tenants on the cathedral estates as no better than his dogs.

In succession to Lynch, Bishop Hoadly installed his own son John, a canon of Winchester of twenty-three years' standing. He rejoiced in his own pluralism, and sounds a most entertaining fellow, much more fun than his earnest father. His passion was amateur theatricals, and he wrote many short plays, farces, and masques. David Garrick dubbed him 'The Rev'd Rigdum Funnidos'. John Hoadly was the author of the verses that appear under the engraved version of Hogarth's *Rake's Progress*. One suspects that he must have found Winchester a little bit sleepy. Gout was his undoing and a generous benefaction to the poor children of Winchester his bequest.

Early in Hoadly's tenure, the hospital nearly lost one of its more interesting architectural features, when a commission was set up to consider the state of the ambulatory. On 25 January 1763 the new bishop of Winchester issued a licence to pull down the 'gallery', which had become 'burthensome and useless and . . . not of any advantage to the said Master or any of the brethren.' Fortunately the project was not carried out. There is scarcely more to report during the tenure of Beilby Porteus, already chaplain to the king, who was appointed master in 1776, a post that he retained when he was consecrated bishop of Chester the same year. He enjoyed a growing reputation as a fine preacher. On his appointment to the see of London in 1787 he resigned the mastership. During his tenure he extended the brothers' graveyard into the south-east angle of the hospital precincts.

The early brothers of St Cross were shadowy figures: we know their names and that is about all. From the eighteenth century onwards a few anecdotes fill out the picture. There was, for example, Brother Robert Bartholomew, buried in January 1771. He had been a soldier during the reign of Queen Anne and was present at the capture of Gibraltar in 1704. For many years he served as the porter, and his portrait used to hang in the

▲ Portrait of Brother Bartholomew, who died in 1771, aged over ninety.

porter's lodge. He was over ninety when he died, though perhaps not 102 as was later written on the back of the painting.

Brother Richard Hart, who died in 1790, was more eccentric, as was recalled many years later by a senior brother who as a child had known the old man: 'He was interred in a coffin of cedar, made by himself twenty years since, out of a plank of a Spanish man-o'-war, which he purchased while a carpenter at Plymouth dockyard. He had written many texts of Scriptures and religious verses on the outside. He kept it constantly in his room, drawn up by pulleys to the ceiling over the window.'

The next master, John Lockman, was a royal appointment (1788); by then presentation to the mastership was done alternately by the archbishop of Canterbury and the king. This seems to have come in because so many masters were, or became, bishops whilst in office. Early in his tenure the hospital was visited by the antiquary John Carter,

who was at that time travelling the length and breadth of England gathering sketches which would be worked up in various publications. His most ambitious project, *The Ancient Architecture of England*, was never completed. Some nineteen of his scrapbooks, filled with drawings ranging from the merest sketches to the most accomplished watercolours, are to be found in the British Library. Amongst these documents is his plan of the hospital precincts (see page 93), which, though crude, contains invaluable information about the layout both of the church and the domestic buildings.

The plan was drawn at a crucial time in the hospital's architectural history. On 6 June 1789 the bishop issued a faculty. It explained that, though the foundation had been built for thirty-five brethren and three sisters, there were now only three brethren lodged and maintained in the hospital, which seemed to have been the case for about 250 years. The apartments on the south side of the great court were uninhabitable. Removing them would add to the 'wholesomeness' of the place, admitting sunlight into the courtyard and adding to the dryness of the buildings.

Carter's plan remains the principal record of this vanished wing. The brothers' apartments were evidently similar to those that survive, and were served by the Lockburn which, after the demolition of the south range, was diverted away from the quadrangle. One interesting feature, that was confirmed during the preliminary archaeological investigation in 2009 for a disability ramp, was a porch allowing direct access from the easternmost flats into the south aisle of the church. Also discovered during that excavation was a deep, stone-lined cistern. It seems to have been intended as a soakaway, receiving water from the inner roof slope of the south range. It had been adapted in the nineteenth century to catch additional water from the church roof. It may have been possible to draw water from it for washing, watering of plants, and so on.

In 1792 the hospital's brewhouse, which stood close to the banks of the Itchen, was pulled down by episcopal licence, as being greatly in excess of requirements. It is shown on John Godson's 1750 plan (page 50) as a very large building indeed, and was undoubtedly medieval. It had been upgraded by John de Campeden, who *c.*1392 installed a large

◀ A FLEMISH TRIPTYCH
DONATED BY MASTER JOHN
LOCKMAN.

new 'furnace', presumably the brewhouse vat, and rebuilt one aisle so as to include a watercourse that flowed through a channel within the building. Now it was to be taken down and a new brewhouse set up in the Hundred Menne's hall. An additional advantage was put to the bishop: the view of St Catherine's Hill would be improved, and it would be possible to enlarge the riverside walk known as The Grove.

Lockman is also remembered at St Cross for his gift to the hospital of a triptych by an unknown artist of the school of the Flemish painter Pieter Coecke Van Aelst (1502–50). Its subject is traditionally called 'The Rest on the Flight into Egypt: Mary, Joseph, and the Infant Jesus on their flight from the persecution of King Herod'. Coincidentally, a somewhat similar triptych is displayed in the Langton Chapel of Winchester Cathedral, on loan from St Michael's Church, Basingstoke. During the nineteenth century the St Cross triptych hung from the east wall of the Brethren's Hall, but is now displayed behind the altar of the south-east chapel.

▶ SPEAKER CORNWALL'S MONUMENT IN THE SOUTH AISLE.

Inevitably, Lockman was an absentee master. He was also a canon of St George's, Windsor, where from around 1750 he lived in Canons' Cloister on the north side of the chapel. He therefore let out the Winchester master's house to the Speaker of the House of Commons, Charles Wolfran Cornwall, whose monument is a prominent feature of the south nave aisle of St Cross Church.

At the very end of the eighteenth century, John Milner provided a final snapshot. The entire population of the hospital comprised 'ten residing brethren, and three out-pensioners, exclusive of one chaplain and the master.' Certain doles of bread continued to be distributed to the poor of the neighbourhood, and 'perhaps the only vestige left in the kingdom of the simplicity and hospitality of ancient times, the porter is daily furnished with a certain quantity of good bread and beer, of which every traveller or other person whatsoever, that knocks at the lodge and calls for relief, is entitled to partake gratis.' Wisely, perhaps, he forebore from passing comment on the thorny issue of the master's emoluments and the stormy debates that were about to arise.

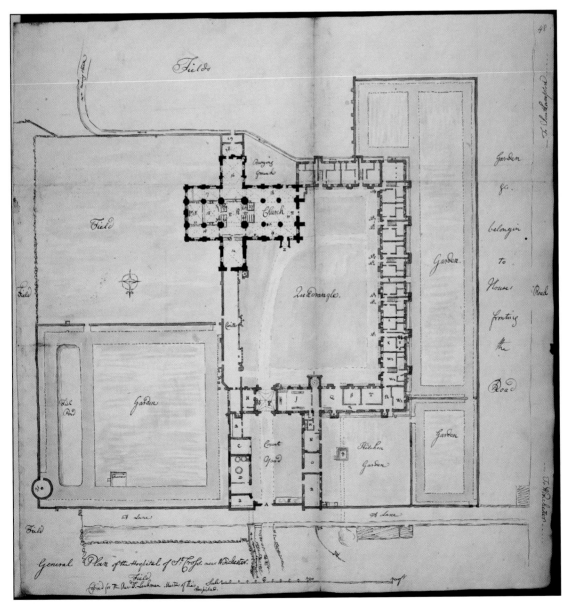

▲ A 'GENERAL PLAN OF THE HOSPITAL OF ST. CROSS NEAR WINCHESTER' BY THE ANTIQUARY JOHN CARTER, 1789.

93

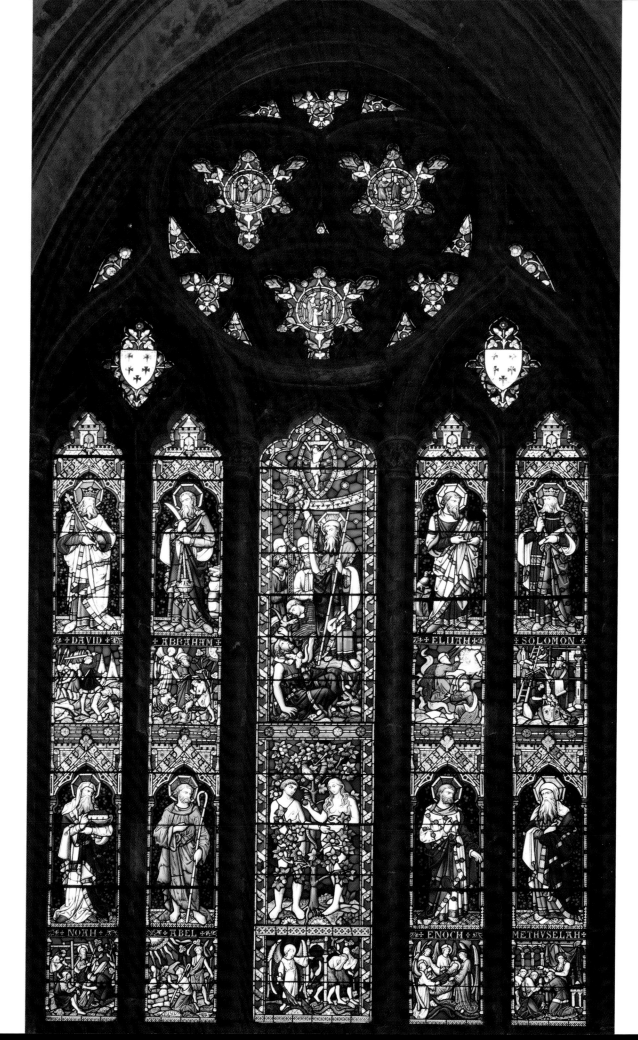

Chapter 8

The Hospital Reformed: The Nineteenth and Early Twentieth Centuries

Governance

The story of the financial irregularities at the hospital during the first half of the nineteenth century has cast a long shadow. At first sight there are parallels with the situation in the fourteenth century, when successive masters were accused of filling their own pockets with revenue intended for the upkeep of the brothers. This issue was closely linked to the question of whether St Cross Hospital was a sinecure benefice. The question emerged again in the late Georgian period: for authors such as Macky and Defoe the fat income of the master was the most memorable feature of St Cross.

Even John Keats was drawn into the debate. His poem *Ode to Autumn* was composed in the Itchen water meadows in September 1819; there is no political polemic in it, but in a contemporary letter to his brother George he commented that the hospital was 'a very interesting old place, both for its Gothic tower and alms-square and for the appropriation of its rich rents to a relation of the Bishop of Winchester'. A few years later, William Cobbett wrote in similar vein in one of his 'Rural Rides',

What is seen at the Hospital of Holy Cross now? Alas! Ten poor creatures creeping about in this noble building, and three out-pensioners; and to those an attorney from Winchester carries, or sends, weekly, the few pence, whatever they may be, that are allowed them! But the place of the 'Master' is, as I have heard, worth a round sum annually. I do not know exactly what it is; but, the post being a thing given to a son of the Bishop, the reader will easily imagine that it is not a trifle.

Another author who is always mentioned in any discussion of the hospital in the nineteenth century is Anthony Trollope. To claim that Hiram's Hospital of *The Warden* (1855) was based on St Cross is an exaggeration. He actually cites the on-going Chancery case at St Cross in contradistinction to the fictional situation in Barchester. He undoubtedly borrowed some elements for his novel, but the hospital he conjured up was a late medieval secular foundation, more like Christe's Hospital in Winchester, founded by the merchant Peter Symonds. There was at St Cross no internal revolution involving disgruntled brethren. The financial irregularities, especially the large amounts of money paid to the warden as a result of increased revenues from property, must have occurred in many other similar institutions.

The whole dispute should be seen in the general context of the Church of England in the eighteenth and early nineteenth century, when malpractices such as simony and pluralism were rife, abuses that it was hoped would be solved by the Ecclesiastical Commission of the 1830s. The issue at St Cross might indeed have been sorted out internally by a self-denying ordinance, but there were those who were determined to bring everything out into the open and effect a purge once and for all.

As we have seen, the seeds of the problem were sown when Abraham Markland composed the Custumary. The arrangement encapsulated within that document worked reasonably well so long as the income remained stable, but by the Georgian period large revenues were being generated from the premiums ('fines') paid for the renewal of leases, when the master was able to pocket the lion's share, with a very small proportion being allotted to the brothers, and minimal returns for the hospital thereafter. Master Lockman was already worried about the disparity between his income and that of the brothers, and in 1792 had taken legal advice. There were particular concerns about granting leases for multiple 'lives', a procedure whereby a lease did not expire until the death of the last surviving individual named in the agreement, typically the principal lessee's youngest son. The ecclesiastical judge Sir William Wynne was of the opinion that leasing the hospital property on lives was unjustified, and advised him to refer the Custumary to the Chancery Court. Lockman, unwisely as it turned out, rejected this advice.

At Lockman's death in 1808 the right to present the master was again in the hands of the bishop, Brownlow North, who put forward his son, Francis. He considered, no doubt, that the addition of the mastership would round out the younger North's portfolio of four livings and a prebendal stall in the cathedral. Perhaps in order to prevent accusations of pluralism, any reference to the care of souls was carefully omitted from the letter of institution, as though the mastership were a secular appointment.

Nevertheless, Francis North may, like Lockman before him, have been uneasy about the terms of the Custumary, and at his appointment added £6 5s 0d to the annual pay of the brothers, a concession echoed by Trollope in *The Warden*, where Septimus Harding increased the statutory stipend by 2d a day. There is no doubting the sincerity of North's attempts at improving the poor men's lot, including spending at least £6,000 on improvements to their living quarters, but this was not enough to spare him from criticism, as Keats and Cobbett made clear. Furthermore, the master's income was rapidly increasing, thanks to even greater fines being granted when leases were renewed. Whereas

the income from rents, which remained low, went to the hospital, the fines continued to increase, particularly when leases for multiple lives were granted, and by far the largest proportion went to the master.

An opportunity for reform might have come with the creation of the Ecclesiastical Commission, but the Commissioners merely noted that the income of the hospital suffered as a result of leasing on lives, making no suggestions as to how the situation might be remedied; the hospital was being run according to the Custumary, and that sufficed. The local press was less accommodating, and the articles that *The Hampshire Independent* published in the 1840s pre-figure the attack made on the Barchester warden by Trollope's imaginary *Jupiter*. The hospital was in the process of renewing the lease of its substantial properties at Crondall. It was announced that 'The fine paid or to be paid is nearly £13,000, the whole of which is to be paid to the Master and Brethren for the time being, the master getting no less than £10,706 for his share of the spoil!'

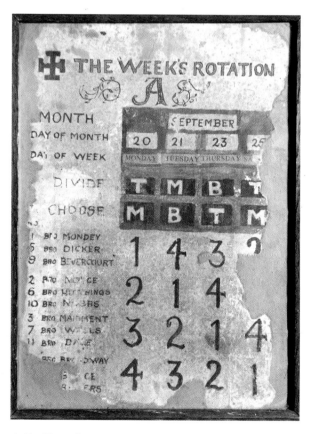

▲ THE 'ROSTER' CONTROLLING THE DISTRIBUTION OF MEAT AT MEAL-TIMES.

A second issue emerged at around this time. A retired clergyman, Henry Holloway, came to live in St Faith's parish and immediately began to question the legal status of St Cross Church, which had served as the parish church since around 1507. Francis North, who by now had inherited the title of Sixth Earl of Guilford and was resident mainly at Alresford, having given up his cathedral prebend, had always maintained that the mastership of the hospital was a sinecure benefice. Amongst the evidence produced at the Chancery case was a letter he had written to his chaplain in 1832 stating that 'The Mastership of St Cross Hospital is not an ecclesiastical benefice. I was appointed to the Hospital merely as Guardian and have no cure of souls, nor was I inducted into the Church which is a Chapel belonging to the institution. I am not subject to ecclesiastical jurisdiction or residence.'

Finally in 1849 the question of St Cross was raised in parliament, and the Commons voted that an enquiry should be set up, which would have involved Guilford in proceedings in the Chancery Court. The earl offered to resign the mastership, but Bishop Sumner, wanting to sort out the problem permanently, refused to accept his resignation. In a desperate bid to avoid Chancery proceedings Guilford attempted to assert that the mastership was an ecclesiastical benefice after all, but the weight of evidence proved the contrary.

In 1853 the Attorney-General produced his assessment: the Custumary was utterly flawed, the master and brethren were guilty of gross breach of trust, the hospital was a lay foundation, and a new scheme must be established to run its affairs. Guilford was ordered to repay such leases and fines that he had obtained since the start of the enquiry. Two years later the bishop accepted his resignation.

Unfortunately the Chancery verdict did not settle the question of the status of the parish of St Faith. Again, the Revd Henry Holloway, who since 1853 was a churchwarden of St Faith's, began to agitate, perhaps providing Trollope with a model for John Bold in *The Warden*. He stirred up the parishioners, telling them that all marriages celebrated in St Cross Church since Guilford's institution were technically invalid, given his lay status. On one occasion he dramatically occupied the church's pulpit and read a prepared statement demanding that the deputy chaplain produce an episcopal licence to perform services there on behalf of the parish. He then exercised his right as churchwarden. 'I interdict you', he told the deputy chaplain, 'from performing any public worship of parochial duty (save baptisms in cases of emergency) within the church or parish of St Cross Hospital and St Faith, or in any building or place within the said united parishes, until specially licensed by the Lord Bishop of the Diocese.' The

◀ THE COKE CART, USED IN THE NINETEENTH CENTURY TO TRANSPORT FUEL TO THE BROTHERS' ROOMS.

bishop soon responded by obtaining an injunction forbidding Holloway from interfering with services at St Cross, and matters became increasingly messy when the local paper implied that Holloway was pursuing a personal vendetta against Guilford and published leaked material to prove it, but to the locals Holloway remained a hero. The joint parochial status of St Cross and St Faith's was recognised.

In 1855 a provisional Scheme for the running of the hospital was drawn up, slightly modified two years later when the first permanent statutes were established. Although there have been some minor changes, the hospital's present constitution was in its broad essentials established at this time. The most significant feature of the 1855 Scheme was that the charity (by which at this stage was meant the original hospital and not Beaufort's Almshouse, then defunct) should be placed under the control of a board of fourteen trustees. They first met in April 1857. Ex-officio trustees comprised the master of St Cross, the dean of Winchester, the mayor of Winchester, the warden of Winchester College, and the rector of Compton; they were balanced by other Hampshire notables. The hospital's income was henceforth to be tightly controlled; leases upon lives were forbidden, as was the imposition of a fine when a lease was granted. The master was to

reside in the hospital, taking over the duties of the former chaplain, and officiate as the incumbent of the parish of St Faith. The brethren were to number thirteen, as originally laid down by Henry of Blois. They must be 'poor, impotent men, having attained the age of fifty years at the least, and not in receipt of parochial relief'. They were to be housed, fed (or receive a payment in lieu of food), given a gown each year, and receive a weekly stipend of five shillings. Provision was made for twenty 'hundred-man poor' to receive one shilling a week. It was hoped that when income permitted it would be possible to revive Cardinal Beaufort's Almshouse of Noble Poverty. A secure muniment room was to be installed on the first floor of the Beaufort Tower to house the hospital's documents.

WILLIAM BUTTERFIELD AND THE RESTORATION OF THE CHURCH

The governance of the hospital having been established, attention turned to the restoration of the church, which was sadly dilapidated. The hospital was still in debt, and the sum of £5,666 was outstanding for the Chancery costs. An initial appeal for funds met with little success; even Lord Guilford was asked whether he would like to

▲ Canon Lewis Macnaughten Humbert, the first master under the new Scheme of 1855.

contribute a communion chalice, a request that met with little sympathy: 'the heavy debt you mention would not exist, had not the Master of the Rolls forced me from my office.'

Despite these financial concerns, William Butterfield was appointed architect for the project. In 1858 he submitted his first report, proposing not mere repair but 'a general refitting' of the nave and choir. The church was still extremely damp, and Butterfield recommended creating a void beneath the floor by taking up the medieval tiles, excavating the earth, and building sleeper walls. He also designed new entrance doors to the church, copying the old design as far as possible. The initial phase of works cost £650, but owing to a shortage of funds major building work ceased from 1860 until 1863. Even so, thanks to the efforts of Master Humbert, the organ by 'Father' Walker was built in the south transept, the blocked windows at the end of the choir were opened up (following the removal of a post-medieval wooden reredos), and Brother King, a former mason, continued the work of removing whitewash and raking out defective pointing inside the church. Later Butterfield had all the walls decorated in a garish mock-medieval painted scheme, which proved so unpopular that it was removed in the 1920s. The shadow of Butterfield's wall painting is still visible in places.

On 14 August 1863 a mysterious envelope arrived on the master's breakfast table. It had

◀ Butterfield relaid salvaged medieval tiles in the nave aisles, including a symmetrical array of modern memorial stones.

been posted in Cowes, and a covering letter asked Lewis Humbert to forward the main missive to the trustees. The writer, who signed himself 'Z.O.', said that on a recent visit to St Cross he had regretted the pause in the restoration work, and was offering an anonymous gift of £500 subject to certain conditions. The money should be applied to the restoration of the east wall of the chancel according to the architect's design, including four new stained glass windows over the high altar which, ideally, should include the initials of Queen Victoria, the late Prince Albert, Bishop Sumner, and the master. Old glass should be removed and placed elsewhere in the church. The monumental brasses within the choir should be reset, and old encaustic tiles should be relaid in their original configuration in parts of the church least susceptible to traffic, such as within the communion rails. The trustees referred these detailed requests to Butterfield, who urged a judicious approach in the treatment of the east end; he also considered that it would be a pity to relay worn out medieval tiles within the chancel; he thought they might best be placed in the aisles where there was also little traffic. Presumably these comments were forwarded to 'Z.O.', who in mid-October wrote from London to say that £500 had been paid into Deane's Bank in the names of the trustees. Subsequently 'Z.O.' made a further

▲ FLOOR TILES IN THE CHOIR BY MINTON COMMEMORATING THE GIFT OF 'Z.O.'

donation of £250, to be devoted to a new west window (he even specified that Wailes and Co of Newcastle should carry out the work), and to resetting any ancient glass in that window elsewhere in the church. 'Z.O.'s munificence was celebrated by Minton tiles in the chancel bearing those initials; speculation has continued to this day as to his identity. It is usually suggested that the donor was Edward Prince of Wales, who had certainly paid a formal visit to St Cross in December 1862. It is supposed that he was on his way to Osborne House on the Isle of Wight, and it has therefore been suggested that 'Z.O.' stands for *zu Osborne*.

Other benefactors joined 'Z.O.' and gradually the repair works were able to go ahead. The church opened again for worship on 19 October 1865. Bishop Sumner preached, taking his text from the prophet Haggai: 'The glory of this latter house shall be greater than the former . . .' After the service a banquet was served to brothers and benefactors in the Brethren's Hall. There was more to do: the very next day Mr Melville Portal opened a fund which was devoted to Butterfield's controversial wall decoration. In 1868 the first 'St Cross Fête' was held, which since then has been an annual fund-raising event, though from an early date the takings have supported the work of St Faith's parish rather than the hospital. Thanks to individual and community efforts the church was brought to its present condition.

One other item of church furniture made its appearance at this time. This is the lectern that is often pointed out as a medieval feature. It is claimed to have an eagle's body and a parrot's head, and is said to have survived the Commonwealth by being sawn in half and buried in a local garden. This is an extraordinary example of the growth of a legend that is impossible to sustain. The lectern is in fact a careful copy of one from St Catherine's Church, Birtles, Cheshire. The original dates from around 1500 and its design derives from metal (latten) lecterns from the Namur region of Belgium; the so-called 'parrot's beak' is simply how eagle heads were imagined at that period. The supposed saw cut is just the normal way such lecterns were made, being carved from two pieces of oak with their grain running in quite different directions: a similar joint occurs in the exemplar at Birtles. The St Cross lectern made its appearance in the 1890s

▲ Late nineteenth-century lectern, a copy of one at St Catherine's Church, Birtles, Cheshire.

when it replaced a rather spindly brass one designed by Butterfield thirty years previously, given in memory of Mr Waddington, an early trustee. It was possibly carved by the local craftsman James Thomas Laverty. Needless to say, this modern piece does not feature in any of the antiquarian literature about St Cross.

When the draft Scheme was put forward in 1855 it included a clear statement that it was not intended to prejudice the possible rebirth of Cardinal Beaufort's foundation. At last, in 1881, the Almshouse of Noble Poverty was reinstated, and once again brothers wearing deep red gowns were seen mingling with those in black (their flat Tudor caps were introduced in 1913). In yet another revision of the Scheme it was enacted that the number of hospital brethren should be maintained between thirteen and eighteen, the Almshouse men to nine. The latter group were initially defined as 'poor men . . . reduced by misfortune from independence to poverty', an approximation to Beaufort's original provision. The minimum entry age for both groups was fifty, but this was subsequently raised to sixty-five for the black brothers and sixty for the red. The minimum age is now sixty for both groups.

▶ St Cross brothers in the late 1860s, by the local photographer William Savage.

Brother Piper.   Brother Griffiths.   Brother King.   Brother Whitebread.

◀ Black and red brothers, 2010.

A description of the running of the hospital in 1836 reveals that the brothers ate in the hall only on Gaudy days and other major church feasts. Otherwise, they collected their meat from the kitchen and took it back to their rooms. This system prevailed throughout the nineteenth century. Because the food was cooked centrally the brothers did not require individual kitchens: the second room at the back of their apartments was a 'scullery', and Butterfield complained on one occasion that the brothers were apt to throw dirty water out of the windows, presumably aiming at the Lockburn beneath. The medieval kitchen remained in use, and was refurbished in 1860 when the wide brick hearth on the north side was rebuilt. The kitchen range and all its equipment was supplied by Josiah Carter, a Winchester ironmonger. It is a delightful tripartite design: on the left a separate fire provided hot water; in the middle, the main hearth has an ingenious way of altering the draft by winding the fire cheeks in and out; there are swivel gallows brackets to suspend pots, a smoke jack, and trivets; and to the right there is a bread oven. Such was state of the art cooking in the mid-nineteenth century.

As Butterfield's work on the church came to an end, the trustees turned their attention to the state

▶ The nineteenth-century fireplace and kitchen range. The bread oven on the right is a partial survival from the fifteenth century.

▲ St Cross brothers, September 1899.

of the brothers' rooms. A rolling repair programme was set up. The work was sensitively done, and the architect respected the design of original features such as the unusual balusters on the staircases, which are cut in a wavy pattern underneath so as to be easier to grip by arthritic hands.

Later in the century new comforts were introduced. Mains drainage was late in coming to Winchester, not least because it was opposed by a group styled the 'Muckabites', who were convinced (rightly, as it turned out) that mains drainage meant higher rates. By 1879 the medieval privies had been plumbed into the main sewer and it was possible to enlarge the hitherto rather small ground-floor privies. Gas lighting was originally installed in the quadrangle in 1870, and in the master's house (still in the north-west corner of the court) the following year, but the brethren's lighting was restricted to candles as a safer option. In 1901 the entire hospital was wired for electricity, but the master maintained a curfew, turning off the mains switch at 10.00 p.m. so that any brother still not in bed would have to resort to candles. This system remained in operation until 1928.

BLOMFIELD, JACKSON, AND THE FIRST WORLD WAR

By the 1890s Arthur Blomfield had replaced William Butterfield, and the trustees commissioned him to work out a scheme for converting the north end of the west range—part of the master's house since Abraham Markland's tenure—back into rooms for the brothers. This meant that a new house had to be designed for the master. William Andrewes hoped that his house would be built in the Master's Garden, but the trustees were unhappy about this idea and eventually it was constructed in the orchard on the north side of the 'Gravels', the approach drive to the hospital. A barn shown on early maps of the area had to be demolished to provide greater space for the garden. Andrewes refused to live in the new house, and the old master's house remained his quarters for four further years until his death in 1903.

By then Sir Arthur Blomfield had died. His architect's practice was kept going by his son Charles, who in 1904 drew up plans for the conversion of the old master's house. By the

▲ Altar of the Memorial Chapel,
by Sir Thomas Graham Jackson.

▲ Statue of St George by Sir George Frampton, part
of Jackson's war memorial.

◀ Sir Charles Nicholson's 'English
altar', showing the fourteenth-
century slab or 'mensa'. Normally
the altar is concealed by a frontal
and altar linen.

time the work was set in hand, the eminent architect Thomas Graham Jackson had taken over. He redrew Blomfield's designs with a few modifications, and in around 1910 the building work was undertaken by John Thompson, the Peterborough building firm that was at that time completing the great work of underpinning and preserving Winchester Cathedral.

Jackson was also the architect for the refurbishment of the north-east chapel as a memorial chapel (appropriately dedicated as the 'Peace Chapel' in 1918) to those killed during the Great War. Jackson designed the chapel's fittings,

including the Portland stone altar and the war memorial on the north side. A vigorous statue of St George by Sir George Frampton stands in a niche between the tablets bearing the names of men of St Faith's parish killed in action.

Minor alterations took place in the church under Sir Charles Nicholson in 1929–30, including the removal of Butterfield's controversial painted decorative scheme. Nicholson was also responsible for remodelling the high altar, incorporating the rediscovered fourteenth-century altar slab and flanking it with curtains supported on riddel posts.

▲ Brethren's Hall and Beaufort Tower in the 1830s, from a drawing by Owen Browne Carter.

Chapter 9

Epilogue
The Hospital in the Modern World

Writers in search of a good story have usually branded St Cross as a remarkable and little-changed survival of a medieval institution, a kind of living fossil in the world of care for the elderly. The present brothers are typically portrayed as the direct descendants of their twelfth-century ancestors, enjoying a life-style that has scarcely changed for nine centuries. This is not really accurate: as we have seen, the hospital has been in continuous evolution since it was first founded. Nevertheless, it remains true that the wonderful buildings survive relatively unchanged precisely because the continued presence of the brothers links our busy modern world with the high middle ages, while the hospital as an institution survives above all because of its ability to adapt to modern conditions. Would St Cross have continued to exist without the amalgamation with St Faith's in the sixteenth century? Through small but significant changes the hospital has managed to provide a service that is still eagerly sought after.

The governance of the hospital is still recognisably similar to that specified in the Scheme of 1855. It is a registered charity, with a board of fifteen trustees. Three of these are *ex officio* members: the master of St Cross, the mayor of Winchester, and the dean of Winchester, so long as they hold those posts. Two trustees are

▶ SOME OF THE BROTHERS.

▶ THE SITTING ROOM OF A
TYPICAL BROTHER'S FLAT.

nominated by Winchester City Council and the
warden of Winchester College respectively; they
are each appointed for a four-year term, renewable
if the nominees desire. The remaining ten trustees
are co-opted and serve five-year terms: one is a
nominee of the parochial church council of St
Faith's. The trustees serve on five committees
with responsibility for finance, fabric, visitors,
welfare, and risk management. The salaried staff
comprise a clerk to the trustees and a deputy clerk,
an accounts manager, a brothers' warden and an
assistant warden, a porter and assistant porter,
a groundsman, a gardener, a maintenance man,
cleaners, and a cook. For architectural matters the
trustees are advised by an architect, a surveyor, an
archaeologist and other specialists.

There are twenty-five brothers in total, seventeen
belonging to the Hospital Foundation (Black
Brothers) and eight to the Foundation of Noble
Poverty revived in 1881 (Red Brothers). There
is now no social distinction between the Red or
Black and each new brother simply joins the same
foundation as his predecessor, into whose flat he
normally moves. The brothers include men from
all walks of life. They must be over sixty and no
longer employed. They are single, divorced, or
widowers: St Cross remains a single-sex institution.
An applicant usually first meets the master or
his deputy, who shows him around the hospital
and answers initial queries. He then completes an
application form and, if fulfilling the criteria, is
invited to spend two days at the hospital, allowing
more time for a discussion of finances with the
clerk to the trustees, an interview with the master
and one of the trustees, and, just as important,
opportunities to meet the brethren. If all goes well
the trustees grant formal approval to the application
at one of their quarterly meetings.

The only obligation is to attend a short daily
service of Mattins, for which gowns are worn. Once
a week comes the 'Pay Parade'; after Mattins the
most junior brother rings a hand-bell from the stairs

▲ RINGING THE BELL FOR THE WEEKLY PAY PARADE.

◀ A FAMILY RECEIVING THE WAYFARER'S DOLE.

of the Brethren's Hall and the brothers assemble to receive the princely sum of one pound, which is tossed over the table in a cloth bag. Like many traditions it is not as old as it seems, having been introduced in 1901.

The brothers' quarters are all in the range of buildings created by Cardinal Beaufort in the fifteenth century. Such was the cardinal's skill in design that the flats still provide ideal accommodation without any significant architectural changes from the original layout. Today's brothers enjoy comforts not available to their medieval predecessors. The open fires have given way to central heating, each bedroom has an en-suite shower room, and individual kitchens are provided. Many brothers prefer, however, to eat their main meal together in a modern dining-room in the north-west corner of the quadrangle.

The Brethren's Hall is still used three times a year for the Gaudy (Latin *gaudeo* : I rejoice), a luncheon attended by the entire hospital community, the trustees, and honoured guests. Gaudies are held at Epiphany, Ascension Day, and Holy Cross Day (14 September).

▶ THE PEACEFUL PRIVATE GARDENS BEHIND THE BROTHERS' RANGE.

The tradition of providing hospitality to people from outside the hospital community continues in various ways, most obviously in the provision of the famous 'Wayfarers' Dole', now a tiny cube of white bread and a small tumbler of beer. More substantial fare is provided in the Hundred Menne's Hall, which serves refreshments during the summer months. The hospital welcomes over 10,000 visitors a year, and many of the brothers are pleased to take both individuals and groups on tours of the church, the Brethren's Hall, and the kitchen. No visit to the hospital would be complete without a walk in the Master's Garden, with its wonderful view of the church reflected in the fish-pond, and the exquisite Compton Garden. At the same time, the layout of the residential buildings fortunately allows the brothers to pursue their lives quietly. Behind the main range are the brothers' own gardens, each provided in the early twentieth century with a shed for storing tools. It is a tranquil spot, where the brothers can indulge in horticulture or sit in the shade of the nodding apple trees heavy with blossom.

St Cross is far from being an introspective community, and benefits in particular from its close association with the parish of St Faith, a link which goes back five centuries. The master of St Cross thus has the unusual distinction of also being priest-in-charge of a parish church (and the present master is also archdeacon of Winchester). The church is in constant use for baptisms, weddings, and funerals, as well as Sunday services and a mid-week service of Holy Communion. The church boasts a fine choir. The hospital also benefits from its link with St Faith's Church of England Primary School, providing a local historical resource that must be the envy of many teachers. Parish involvement also includes the annual St Cross Fête, held at the end of June as a parish rather than specifically hospital event. A recent innovation is the annual 'Knights' Festival' with its jolly jousting fun.

Inevitably, the funding of such an institution is an ongoing concern. Visitors bring in some revenue, but increasingly the trustees look to augment the hospital's income by such ventures as concerts, hire for filming, non-local weddings, and wedding receptions. Even so, the architect's latest quinquennial report on the state of the buildings has highlighted the need for extensive fabric repair, including general repairs to the main buildings and church and the progressive refurbishment of the brothers' flats. Consideration is also being given to enhancing areas of the hospital not currently in use, which might have the potential to be a revenue stream, but the investment will be costly. It is a challenge, but after nearly nine centuries the hospital is used to challenges.

Ask any of the brothers, and he will tell you that the hospital is a vibrant community, a wonderful place to live. It is a hive of activity thanks to the constant influx of visitors. The church is in active parochial use, and is seldom empty: one might find flower arrangers preparing for a wedding or the Sunday services, people polishing brass or woodwork, a choral group practising, or perhaps just a single person at prayer. At the same time, the hospital is a haven of peace, where one can sit in the delightful Master's Garden with its summer flowers nodding against a backdrop of ancient masonry, lulled by the plash of water from the fountain. Autumn inevitably reminds one of Keats and his evocation of the mists that so often fill the Itchen valley in early morning. Winter snows bring enchantment too, when one may wander through the frozen water-meadows with the hospital buildings standing stark against a leaden sky. Then the snowdrops peek through the ground beneath the ancient plane tree in the Master's Garden, a promise of a world that is young once more.

MASTERS OF THE HOSPITAL OF ST CROSS

Before the thirteenth century the names and dates of masters are very uncertain.

*c.*1132	Robert de Limoux		1545	William Meadow
	names unknown		1557	John Leefe
1185	'Roger'		1557	Robert Reynolds
1190	Alan de Sainte-Croix		1559	John Watson
*c.*1212	Alan de Stoke		1583	Robert Bennett
c. 1235	Humphrey de Millers		1603	Arthur Lake
1241	Henry de Susa		1616	Sir Peter Young
1248	Geoffrey de Ferring		1627	William Lewis
*c.*1260	Thomas de Colchester		1649	John Lisle
*c.*1268	Stephen de Wotton		1657	John Cook
1289	Peter Seymour (de Saint-Maur)		1660	Richard Shute
1296	William de Wendling		1660	William Lewis [reinstated]
1299	Robert Maidstone		1667	Henry Compton
1321	Geoffrey de Welford		1676	William Harison
1323	Bertrand d'Assier		1694	Abraham Markland
1333	Peter de Galiciano		1728	John Lynch
1335	William of Edington		1760	John Hoadly
1345	Raymond Pelegrini		1776	Beilby Porteous
1345	Walter de Wetwang		1788	John Lockman
1346	Richard Lusteshall		1808	Francis North
1349	John of Edington		1855	Lewis Humbert
1366	William Stowell		1868	William Andrewes
1368	Richard of Lyntesford		1901	Hon. Alan Brodrick
1370	Roger de Cloune		1909	Francis Causton
1374	Nicholas Wykeham [sequestrator]		1928	Alfred Daldy
1383	John de Campeden		1936	Charles Bostock
1410	John Forest		1943	Oswald Hunt
1426	Thomas Forest		1953	Geoffrey Carlisle
1563	Thomas Chaundler		1970	Kenneth Felstead
1465	William Westbury		1980	Colin Deedes
1473	Richard Harward		1992	Anthony Outhwaite
1489	John Lichfield		2005	James Bates
1492	Robert Sherborne		2009	Michael Harley
1508	John Claymond			
1524	John Incent			

Index

Select Bibliography

Unpublished sources

St Cross Archives, deposited at Hampshire Record Office (hereafter HRO), ref. 111M94W. The catalogue may be viewed via the HRO web site, http://www3.hants.gov.uk/archives

'St Cross Register', also known as *Liber Secundus*. A register compiled before 1409. HRO, 111M94W/C1/1, available as microfiche, HRO Misc. Fiche, 237-40.

'St Cross Cartulary', a late fourteenth-century register, British Library Harley MS 1616, also available as microfilm at HRO, ref. W/K8/8.

Baigent, Francis Joseph, Notes on St Cross, British Library Add MSS 39976.

Curtis, T., 'Condition Survey and proposals for the conservation of the wall paintings', unpubl. conservation report, March 2001.

Harrison, H., St. Cross Church, Winchester, Hampshire, 'The Choirstalls and Morning Chapel Entrance Screen', unpubl. conservation report October 2010.

Kusaba, Y., 'The Architectural history of the church of the Hospital of St. Cross in Winchester and its place in the development of early Gothic architecture', Ph.D. thesis, Indiana University 1983, publ. University Microfilms International (Ann Arbor and London, 1984).

Published Sources

Crook, J., 'The Hospital of St Cross', in M. Bullen, J. Crook, R. Hubbuck, and N. Pevsner, *The Buildings of England, Hampshire: Winchester and the North* (London, 2010), pp. 710-25.

Hopewell, P., *Saint Cross: England's Oldest Almshouse* (Chichester, 1995).

Humbert, L. M., *Memorials of the Hospital of St. Cross and Alms House of Noble Poverty* (Winchester and London, 1868).

Kirby, T. F. (ed.), *Wykeham's Register*, Hampshire Record Soc., 2 vols. (Winchester, 1896–9).

Riall, N., 'The Diffusion of early Franco-Italian *all'antica* ornament: the Renaissance frieze in the chapel of the Hospital of St Cross, Winchester, and the Gaillon stalls, now at St Denis, Paris', *Antiquaries Journal* 88 (2008), pp. 258-307.

Warren, W. T., *St Cross Hospital near Winchester: its History and Buildings* (Winchester, 1899).